SUDDENLY BLIND

D1736059

D. Wermuth

3-13-13

BY DAVID WERMUTH

LCCN# 2012900636
ISBN 10: 0615579949
ISBN-13: 978-0615579948
(Wermuth Publishing, LLC, Brooksville, Florida)

www.suddenlyblind.net
Email: workerbee123@earthlink.net
www.usastickershock.com

ACKNOWLEDGEMENTS

When I began to write this book two years ago, I wasn't sure if I'd ever finish it. In fact it started out only as a way for me to write down my thoughts from my childhood. As I continued to write, it became more difficult. I'm very thankful for those who have put up with me and were there to offer support and encouragement. If it wasn't for them, this book would undoubtedly still be locked away deep in my hard drive.

First, I would like to thank Holly for enduring the nights of me being at my computer and not spending precious time with her. There were many times she rolled over only to hear my computer keys clicking away in the other room.

Also, a special thank you to my sisters, Barbara and Connie, for contributing some memories that have been long locked away and the love you have shown me as your brother. Your voices have been comforting through the years and always uplifting.

Linda Wilder I would also like to thank for all the support you have given from the time I lost my sight. Linda has encouraged me and been there through the thick and thin times.

Thank you Author John Dunn for your inspiration.

A very special thank you to Dr. Rod Yoder for editing - you helped me bring this book to completion.

There are many more people to thank in my lifetime, thank you as well for all the good times and laughs.

CONTENTS

FOREWORD

I met David in 1995 when he applied to receive Rehabilitation Services from Washington State Services for the Blind. I was fortunate to be the Vocational Rehabilitation Counselor assigned to work with him.

David lost his vision just four months before I began my work with him. He was told he would never regain his vision. He did not let this devastating news stop him. He immediately set out to work on developing skills necessary to regain his independence and confidence. David attended and later graduated from the Washington State Orientation and Training Center for adults who are blind. Once he could demonstrate his independence using a white cane, he traveled to Oregon and received his first dog guide.

Along with his initial success, there were problems. David disclosed to me his addiction to alcohol, and there were times when I wondered if he was going to overcome this addiction. In the years to follow, however, he did achieve recovery.

In spite of his problems, David decided to enroll at Pierce Community College to earn a higher degree of education. While working on his AA degree, he became president of Barrier Breakers, an organization for students with disabilities.

David's career goal was to work for a state agency for the blind. In order for him to reach this goal, he needed to obtain a BA degree. He earned this degree at the University of Washington in Tacoma.

Shortly after he graduated, David called me full of excitement to tell me he had been hired as a Rehabilitation Teacher at the Texas Commission for the Blind.

He kept in touch from Texas and we would often consult on his questions regarding his clients. David wanted to be the best teacher in Texas and proudly proclaimed he was. David called me one morning and said he was leaving his job and coming back to Washington. I could tell he didn't want to do this but family issues made it impossible for him to continue his work there.

David and I talked on a weekly basis after his return and although he battled through divorce, he remained in recovery from his alcoholism.

That was over seven years ago. David has kept in touch with me over the years, keeping me up to date about his challenges, adventures and successes.

When David encounters problems in his life, he starts making a plan to work through them and comes out a better man and is ready for the next challenge.

David's past, his resilience for life, and his desire to help people are the characteristics that make it a pleasure to know him.

Linda Wilder, Vocational Rehabilitation Counselor,
Washington State Department of Services for the Blind, January
26, 2011

I CHECKED HIS VITALS; HE'S STILL ALIVE

I violently slammed down the receiver of the phone and cursed my dad. I walked towards my wife Theresa and said, "HOW DARE YOU!"

I then backhanded her across her face as she stared into my angry eyes. She walked to the telephone and called 911. I had had all I could take, and I grabbed my handgun from my bedroom drawer. I went into my bathroom and closed the door.

The Springfield police were dispatched and on their way.

Official Springfield Police Report
Case # 95-3724
April 12, 1995

"At apprx. 16:48 hrs. Officer Rod Harrison and myself were dispatched to 1550 (Q). St. #22 regarding a domestic disturbance. Dispatch advised the involved male and female had been arguing all day and that the dispute had become (physical). Dispatch also advised that there were weapons in the residence but they were in a dresser.

OBSERVATION / INVESTIGATION:
The involved apartment was located upstairs on the southwest corner of the complex. Upon arrival

the front door was found to be open. I could not see anyone within the living room/kitchen area.

Due to the traffic noise from the freeway, I was unavailable to hear anything within the residence.

I knocked and announced "Springfield Police", a female, subsequently identified as T/Theresa Wermuth, walked out of the hallway area (I was unable to see anything but the hallway entrance). I asked the female, "Where is the other subject?"

She nonchalantly replied, "Oh, he is in the bathroom with a gun to his head."

I replied, "He is in the bathroom with a gun to his head?"

She replied, "Yes."

I requested the female subject to exit the residence, she went to a kitchen table and sat down. I angled myself so I could see the bathroom area. I noted the door was partially closed, and I was unable to see into the bathroom area. I then heard the report of a small caliber weapon and the sound of a body fall. I instructed Officer Two to remove the female from the residence and simultaneously requested an ambulance be dispatched (ASAP) to our location.

I then pushed open the bathroom door and observed V/David Wermuth lying on the floor in a puddle of blood. I observed a small chromed handgun behind the bathroom door. This was secured and handed to Officer Two.

V/David Wermuth was lying on his left side, I noted a contact wound to his right temple area (circular powder marks were observable), I was unable to tell if an exit wound was present, checked V/Wermuth for vital signs and found him to be breathing. He subsequently moved his head around so I believed he had limited injuries to his neck. Due to what appeared to be a large amount of blood loss on the left side of V/Wermuth's head I believed an exit wound was present. I slightly elevated the head and slightly applied pressure in an attempt to stop the bleeding. I also applied slight pressure to the contact wound to inhibit bleeding from there. I talked with V/Wermuth explaining to him that the paramedics were in route and that he would "be O.K." He subsequently responded by saying, "I want to die."

He said this several times. I asked, "What could be so bad that you would do this?"

V/Wermuth replied, "*Life.*"

He also stated, "I thought it would kill me."

Springfield paramedics subsequently arrived and took over medical treatment. V/Wermuth was transported to the MC Kenzie/Willamette hospital by s.f.d..."

CHAPTER 1

JULY 25, 1962-DID I REALLY HAVE TO BE BORN?

The very first memory I have of my life is standing over my new electric train set getting a spanking by my dad. I was probably two and a half or three years old. Dad had just bought me the train set and set it up on a piece of plywood in my bedroom. I remember holding the controls and watching it go around in circles. I am not sure what I was thinking, but I stood up, dropped my pants and urinated on it.

My sister Barbara saw me and went running out of my room to tell Dad. I remember his face as he came into my room. Since my pants were already down he took the opportunity to spank my butt. Then he placed me in a corner for what seemed like hours.

I stood there and cried, asking Mom several times if I could come out of the corner, but Dad was at a female neighbor's home again and he had the final word. Mom was on my side to get me out of the corner, and she kept sending Barbara over to the neighbor's place to ask him, but Barbara always came back and told Mom, "Dad said no."

It was the fourth or fifth time when finally she came back and said, "Dad said okay."

The next morning Dad made me take each and every one of the train-set pieces and put them in the outside garbage can. I could only carry one piece at a time, so it took ten or more trips. It was like walking the gauntlet each time I came in or out, because I had to walk by Dad, Mom and Barbara. It worked as a good form of punishment because I felt really ashamed.

It encouraged me to never urinate on train sets, and I haven't to this day.

Dad never bought me another train set no matter how much I threw a tantrum, cried or begged.

I was born the middle child of three children. Barbara was two years older and Connie was one year younger than I.

My father, Donald Edward Wermuth, was a very proud man most of his life. His parents passed away when he was eight years old and he was handed around among his older brothers and sisters until he joined the Air Force at the age of seventeen. By all accounts he had a pretty hard childhood and always longed for a satisfying family life. He didn't speak often about his childhood other than to say, "My brothers and sisters did their best."

My mother, Marsha, was born into a very Italian Catholic family. She was brought up in a very strict but loving home, the middle child of three, with two brothers. Her older brother, Johnny, was born with a slight mental handicap. Jimmy was the baby of the family.

Mom grew up with strong family values. Being the only female child, she helped my grandmother Blanche and grandfather Victor take care of her brothers, which they appreciated.

My father and mother met in 1958 while dancing one Friday night at the Red Roof Inn in Tacoma, Washington. My mother was still in high school and my father was stationed at McCord Air force Base in Tacoma. Mom told me that she fell in love with my father because he was handsome and had a car. He would pull up in his convertible right outside her last class and wait for her. She could see him through the windows.

"Most of my girlfriends were jealous of me and liked him, too," she said.

Mom enjoyed all the attention he gave her and soon she fell even more deeply in love with him, and that love was reciprocated.

They were married in 1960, and my sister Barbara was born a few months later. I was delivered a couple of years later in Everett, Washington, on July 25, 1962.

Dad was reassigned to the Azores in Portugal, and Mom packed us all up while pregnant with Connie, who was born in 1963.

Mom found herself in a strange country and mostly alone with three children. She did have maids helping her and paid only about five dollars a month for full-time help. She had to fire them quite often, because they were so poor that they would steal diapers, milk and other items. The women needed the job, but Mom said that there was an underlying hatred of Americans because we had so much and they had very little.

Dad now had the family he wanted. But Mom soon found out he was also a womanizer. He spent most of his time off work sitting in men's clubs, and he paid for the privilege of sleeping with the women.

Then Dad was transferred to New Mexico, and Mom felt relieved to get back to the United States. We all went with Dad to New Mexico in 1964 and settled there for a little over a year.

Dad was a very hard worker and wanted the best for his children. He had two jobs – working at a Texaco gas station and his job in the Air Force. We kids had everything in the way of toys, a nice home and a family life. Dad took me to his work on occasion, and I always brought something home with "Tony the Tiger" on it: beach towel, semi truck, whatever the promotions were. The pictures taken around Christmas that I saw many years later showed lots of toys for us kids around the tree.

I later heard that my grandmother and grandfather visited us in New Mexico at least once to buy food for our kitchen cupboards. It was quite a long trip for them but they did it because of their love for us. I also learned that they had to bring food to us previously in Everett quite a few times. Dad found it hard to buy food as well as go to the cocktail lounges to pick up women, so he chose the women.

What I remember of New Mexico besides my train set is mostly tumbleweeds and it being so hot. We had friends there our age and one time we had an Easter egg hunt with all the kids in the neighborhood. After the colored egg hunt we all went off and ate the candy and hardboiled eggs in our friends' backyard. I was sitting there unshelling my eggs and our friends' pet dog came up to me. It was a smaller dog and it stood there with its tail wagging. I didn't know better, so I fed the dog all of my eggshells and then ate the eggs.

Barbara and I were asked the next day by Dad, "Who fed the dog eggshells?"

Barbara and I looked at each other and we both said, "Not me."

Dad said, "They took their dog to the vet last night and it died."

Forty years later I still have a picture in my mind of that little dog, with its tail wagging, eating those eggshells.

I wonder if that is why I have such a strong love for dogs to this day.

Did I mention that Dad spent a lot of time at the neighbor's home? Either Mom was naive or she just didn't want to believe it, but Dad told me later that he would go over to the neighbor's, where Mom's girlfriend lived, to have sex.

He also told me when I was in my teenage years, "It happened often, with several women." One occasion that he was especially proud of was the time he got Mom drunk while her friend was over. They were all three drinking and, because Mom didn't drink much, she got tipsy pretty fast and passed out on the couch. Her friend and Dad helped her to bed and then went into the living room. Dad grabbed a blanket and covered up while they had sex on the couch.

Then, he said, as if this was his proudest moment, "Your mom stumbled out of our bedroom and sat down in a chair across from us. She was so drunk she didn't comprehend what we were doing. I yelled at her to go back to bed and she did. We finished and the friend went home."

The next morning Mom either didn't remember or didn't care about it; she never said a word.

I also remember getting on the train many times with Mom and my sisters and going back to Washington State to stay with my grandma and grandpa. We kids didn't know it but our family was falling apart because my father was very proud to have his family, but he just couldn't keep his pants up.

There was also this little war going on in Vietnam and Dad was called to duty. We three kids being so young didn't understand what that really meant. All we knew was that Dad was going to be gone for awhile, so we got on the train and looked forward to seeing Grandma and Grandpa.

CHAPTER 2

I LOVE MY GRANDMA AND GRANDPA

When we returned to Tacoma we moved in with Grandpa and Grandma. They had a three-story house with two bedrooms in the basement. Uncle Jimmy slept in one and I slept in the other. Grandpa and Grandma used the bedroom on the main floor. Barbara and Connie slept upstairs in one of two bedrooms and the other one was for Uncle Johnny. Mom slept on the couch, when she was there.

To start the day off, Grandma would cook breakfast for us three kids. Usually we had oatmeal, toast and juice, and occasionally cold cereal. The oatmeal breakfast was my favorite. Grandma put vanilla in it and cinnamon on our toast.

Barbara went off to school every day and Connie stayed home and played. I had a friend across the street and we played together most of the afternoon.

One day I was in trouble for doing something and didn't get to go outside. The next day, when I asked Grandma if I could go play with my friend, she told me he was in the hospital. She said it was a good thing we hadn't been together the day before because he got his legs run over by a car. He and I always sat on the curb and talked. That day a car had pulled up and run over his legs, breaking both of them.

That was the last time I ever saw my friend, so it may have been worse and they didn't want to tell me. I'm guessing that he probably lost both his legs and they didn't want me to see him.

Grandpa was a sheet metal technician on McCord Air Force Base. Early each afternoon Barbara came home from school and then we waited for Grandpa to get back from work. We had Grandma keep a lookout for him and tell us when he pulled into the driveway.

Barbara, Connie and I then hid in the dining room closet, covering ourselves up with coats or blankets and listening for him to come in the door. We always heard him ask, "Where are the kids?"

Grandma always said, "They're hiding and they want you to find them."

Bless his heart! Grandpa would put down his lunch pail after a long day's work and come looking for us. He started in the kitchen, opening the cabinets and closing them loudly saying, "Nope, not in here. Where are them kids?"

He would do this for quite awhile, and it was hard not to giggle and let him hear us. The closer he got to our closet, the wider our eyes opened with excitement. He always took his time, so our excitement built.

Then he would open the closet door and say, "I found you!" and hug all three of us.

I loved my grandma and grandpa, because they always dropped what they were doing and played with us when we wanted.

Grandpa and Grandma never laid a hand on us, and Grandpa only yelled at me once. When I was three or four I was a biter. I would wait until Grandma was doing dishes and then I would sneak up on her. She always wore dresses and I'd come up behind her and bite her pretty hard on her thigh or calf. She would scream out in pain. I thought it was funny.

The last time I bit Grandma was when Grandpa came into the kitchen and yelled, "*You ever do that again and I'll blister your butt!*"

I went to the couch and pouted for quite a long time. But I never bit her again.

Grandpa's mother was still living. We met her only once. She had Alzheimer's disease and was hospitalized and passed away shortly after that visit.

Grandma's parents, John and Mary, were still living and we went there for the holidays. My great-grandfather John was tall and lanky, and he dressed kind of like Abraham Lincoln. He, too, never raised his voice, and we could tell he loved us. He never said much but we'd sit on his lap while he told us stories.

My great-grandmother Mary was shorter, and a large woman. We called her "Big Grandma" and Grandma "Little Grandma" to let others know who we were talking about.

They lived in Sumner, Washington, and had some property with a large garden on it. My great-grandmother was a good cook. All our holiday meals were made from scratch: bread, pasta, dessert and all the vegetables fresh from the garden. We would walk into their home and smell the freshly baked bread. We never left there hungry.

We played with our cousins after meals so the adults could play cards. One time Connie and I played sword fighting with long sticks. Nearby there was a barrel in which trash was burning, and we decided to get the tips of our swords hot. That was fun for a while but when we wanted to play something else, we dropped our swords onto the dry grass and went to another part of their property. We came back a while later and, sure enough, there was a fire truck there putting out the grass fire. They must not have suspected that we lit the fire because they never asked us. Perhaps they just thought that a hot ember had blown out of the barrel. Or maybe they knew that we did it but thought, "Kids will be kids."

Our great-grandfather passed away first, and Big Grandma died about six months later from natural causes.

Grandma and Mom said she passed away from a broken heart. This happens often Mom told us; they were together most of their lives and she wanted to be with him even in death.

My dad came back from Vietnam and apparently Mom and Dad were not going to stay together. Dad picked us up every so often and took us to a motel called The Rose in Tacoma. He wanted to get the family back together, but Mom had gotten tired of his womanizing and physical abuse. He would threaten not to bring us back and Grandpa would have to go hunt us down.

I always looked forward to seeing Dad because he spoiled us. I also liked staying at the motel and going out to eat and getting to pick what I wanted off the menu. He had money so he'd buy us each a toy, and I usually ended up picking out a new gun or rifle of some sort.

Dad volunteered for another tour of duty in Vietnam later, telling me he had to get the extra combat pay so the bill collectors couldn't chase him. "Your mom ran the credit bills up so high, I had to go back," he told me.

We moved out of Grandma and Grandpa's home and into our own. We moved quite frequently until we landed on East I Street in Tacoma.

It wasn't long after we moved in that we were hurried over to our neighbors across the street. We went into their home and I noticed a shotgun perched up against the wall by the front door. There were race riots going on close by and we had to spend the night there. I saw boxes of ammunition sitting on the kitchen table. Our neighbor was sitting there with a shotgun across his lap, and he got up every so often to look out the window.

I heard him say, "Look at them animals. If they try to come in here I'll give each and every one of them a round."

The next thing I remember is hearing glass breaking and bullets going off outside. I wanted to look but they sent us to bed. I was very scared.

The next day we went home and the riots calmed down. I heard Mom talking about it, saying, "Even the cops wouldn't stop. They just sped away."

We had moved to this house in the middle of summer, and Grandpa and Grandma bought us a brand new swimming pool for our backyard. The neighborhood kids would come over and we had lots of friends. Mom babysat at our home for extra money because she was on public assistance. I remember two families of kids in particular.

The first were two girls our ages. Their dad would drop them off and pick them up. He wanted his girls to learn to swim but Mom couldn't afford the swimming lessons for us three. He ended up paying for all five of us to have swimming lessons, and that's how I learned to swim that summer.

One of the girls and I had a fondness towards each other, and it wasn't long before we were playing "Doctor" whenever we could hide and get away with it. We were just exploring each other's body parts like kids do who are curious about the opposite sex. She let me experience her different female body parts with my hands and she would lie there touching my penis, giggling as I grew an erection.

One day she and her sister didn't show up. I'm guessing she must have told her daddy and off they went.

The second family of kids my mom babysat also had two girls my age, as well as a boy who was too young to participate in any playing. Their father, Perk, was raising them on his own.

Mom and Perk would frequently get us six kids a sitter on the weekends and they would go out dancing. Perk attempted to take on the role of my dad and tried very hard to fill the role of a husband as well. He loved my mom and when he passed away twenty years later, he still had a picture of her in his wallet. I liked Perk, and Janice, his oldest daughter, was exactly my age. Cara, his second daughter, was one year younger and Barney was two years younger.

I turned five that summer and enjoyed riding my new bike and getting more independent. I am not sure how many times I didn't look before I rode my bike across one of the busy roads by our house, but I should have been hit by cars several times. I'd come flying out of the 7-Eleven store right into the road, hear cars slam on their brakes, and usually someone would get rear-ended. I was the favorite kid of the body repair shops in my neighborhood. Karma will get you; a car once stopped to avoid hitting a child and, lo and behold, I was behind it and rear-ended it. I was really glad at least the child didn't get hurt.

Mom was struggling financially but most of the time seemed to have enough food to feed us, though not always food we liked. In those days kids usually didn't get an option about what they wanted. What was on the table was what you ate or you'd go to bed hungry. About once a week Perk came in with hamburgers, fries and a soft drink while picking up his kids, and we all ate together. It was always a nice surprise because that usually wasn't in our budget.

When we went to visit my grandma and grandpa once a week, Grandma usually gave us three kids a dollar or two each to stop at McDonald's.

One time she gave us two dollars each and said, "Go to McDonald's and get your dinner."

Mom stopped at a McDonald's on the way home and, while we were getting out of the car she said, "Connie, you get four Cokes. Barbara, you get four French fries, and David, you get one cheeseburger and three hamburgers."

Mom wanted me to buy only one cheeseburger because we couldn't have cheeseburgers until we turned seven years old.

I always asked for a cheeseburger, but Mom said, "They cost more. No."

Barbara and Connie bought what they were supposed to and I told them I was going to buy what I wanted, so I went to the counter and ordered a quarter pounder with cheese, large fries and a Coke.

When I jumped into the car, Barbara and Connie had already spilled the beans to Mom. She took our change and bought Barbara and Connie a hamburger, then took my quarter pounder and ate it. I sat at the table when we got home and ate a bowl of cereal; I received a spanking and then I was sent to bed. I put up an argument that I was "the man of the house," but to no avail. Mom was the boss.

I was also introduced to the wooden spoon that night. She carried that wooden spoon with her from then on. I think she used to practice pulling it out of her purse like a gunslinger, because you didn't even see it coming upside your head.

In the car Mom had us three sit in the back seat most of the time, and even with the littlest argument from us, you'd barely see her hand with that wooden spoon in it hit you, usually across the forehead. She hit me one time and it cut my head. Blood was dripping down my face. She had to pull into the hospital emergency room and rush me in. I tried to get her in trouble with the doctor but to no avail. He passed it off as an accident. Back in those days you could almost kill your kid and just say they had it coming, and get away with it.

Mom babysat Janice, Cara and Barney through the rest of the summer, and then it was time for me to start kindergarten.

CHAPTER 3

DAD, WILL YOU COME BACK, PLEASE?

Grandma took Barbara and me to buy new school shoes before school started. Connie wasn't old enough yet so I'm not sure if she got shoes or not. However, here I was walking to school a couple of blocks away from our house with my new shoes on. I was carrying my rug and pillow for nap time. Barbara was now in second grade. Janice walked with us too and – yahoo! – she was in my class.

I liked school because there were so many kids to play with and the lunches were good.

Janice and I passed notes at recess and I chased her around along with the other girls. She and I became boyfriend and girlfriend and sometimes even held hands on the playground. She wore dresses, and we boys waited by the monkey bars to look up her dress and those of the other girls as they climbed across.

At that time we got our clothes from Goodwill, and I always got picked on or made fun of. Poor Barbara and Connie had to wear "cat-eye" glasses. I am not sure where Mom got them but, boy, did they make my sisters look funny. Now and then Mom permed their hair and all I could do was laugh. They would be so embarrassed and hate to go anywhere. I didn't have to worry about her messing my hair up; she just buzzed my head, which I hated.

Dad started coming to get us on his visitation for the weekend and taking us to his home in Puyallup, Washington. The first time we went to his house we were amazed. He had a brand new home, brand new cars in his driveway and a beautiful speedboat.

We were also introduced to his new wife, Mary, and our new half-sister, Debbie. Mary was always nice to us and even let Mom babysit Debbie for extra money for a short time. That all ended when Mom called Mary, telling her Dad kept trying to sleep with her when he picked up Debbie.

Dad even tried to give Mom a car to drive because we always had clunkers, but Mary put a stop to it saying, "Let her buy her own car."

One car we had was several different colors. The back floors were rusted through, and you had to be careful not to put your feet in certain areas. Barbara usually sat up front by now as she was the oldest. Connie and I dropped stuff through the floor as Mom drove and then, from the back window, watched it appear on the road. Connie and I also played "love bug" and punched each other in the arm. The first person to see a Volkswagen called out "love bug" and got one punch. I usually looked out for the Volkswagens more than Connie and punched her more than she punched me. One time I punched her too hard and she dropped my shoe through the floor.

She was laughing as we looked out the back window and watched the shoe disappear in the distance.

That car didn't have very good door locks. One evening we were driving down a dirt road with all three of us in the back, Connie to the right of me and Barbara to my left. I was talking to Barbara and when I turned to talk to Connie all I saw was an empty seat with the door cracked open.

I turned to Barbara and said, "Where's Connie?"

Barbara looked and screamed, "Mommy, Connie fell out of the car!"

Mom slammed on the brakes frantically and we went back to find her. Connie was standing on the side of the dirt road with a look on her face as if she wondered what had taken so long for us to come back. But she wasn't hurt. She just had some small pebbles embedded in her.

After that Connie had to sit in the middle between Barbara and me. I always liked Dad's cars better because I didn't have to worry about the door opening while going around corners and falling out.

It was always a fun time going to Dad's home. Dad always had something for us to do. We were either on the lake in his boat, going out to eat, or even having a nice family meal at their home.

There was a large swampy wooded piece of property behind his home and we explored for fun. My favorite adventure would be to find little snakes. Barbara and Connie would usually be playing in the backyard, I'd run at them with the snake until they went running into the house screaming. One day I lost track of time and Dad came looking for me. He wasn't happy and I lost my privilege to go off on my own. This lasted a couple of years. Then before we knew it, Mary and Debbie went back home to Montana and Dad sold his house. We moved as well to a largely Black area of Tacoma.

I hardly went outside unless it was to school. I wouldn't go to school in that neighborhood – there was no way I was going to be the only white boy attending a Black school. I remembered the riots a year earlier. Connie and I were already having to fight the Black kids in the neighborhood often, and why would I want to go to school with "animals," as my neighbor called them? So we took the bus to a white school about ten miles away.

First grade was fun to go to and I was able to make friends. We played marbles at recess and I held my own.

By this time food was getting scarce at our house. There was usually something, but eating Hamburger Helper or beans and ham all the time was pretty tiresome. I'm sure there was a bit more variety than that, but I remember those vividly and hated them when they were served. We went to school early so we could eat school breakfasts, and I always ate my free lunch, because it was better than what Mom was cooking.

Dad always made fun of Mom's cooking when we went to visit him, saying, "All she could cook was eggs and she burned them. I ate eggs for breakfast, lunch and dinner."

Of course I'd tell her what he had said.

Her favorite comeback was, "You tell that idiot…" In my early years, I thought Dad's name was "Idiot."

It was about this time that I began to notice that Mom picked on Connie quite a bit and went out of her way to embarrass and shame her. My grandfather Victor became sick around this time. He would have put a stop to the abuse we were getting, but he didn't know about it. He passed away in December of 1969 from a brain tumor. I loved my grandpa and only wish he could have lived longer to protect us.

Grandma had a very beautiful funeral for Grandpa and it seemed as though half of Tacoma attended and paid their respect. Grandpa was a very liked person and didn't have a mean bone in his body.

The rest of our family either turned a blind eye to mom's abuse or didn't know what was going on. I'm sure that they felt powerless to stop it, and we became less involved in family outings. Uncle Jimmy, when he had time from work or college, would come get us three and give mom a break. Jimmy and Jan, his girlfriend, took us with their family to the ocean for some weekends, into their home, and Jimmy even took me to his work a few times.

Jimmy had a side business while he was going to college taking loads of junk to the dump for his customers. I remember one day Jimmy and I went to an auto glass shop and filled his truck four times and he was paid ten dollars a load. It was a hot day and after two loads of going to the dump the guard at the dump asked if this was his personal glass. Back in those days if you were dumping your personal trash it was free, but if it was a business you had to pay to dump. Jimmy said, "Yes, it's mine," then he would hand them a cold Coke and they would let us through without paying. Jimmy paid me two dollars a day and at that time that was quite a bit of money for me. I loved working for him and he would always buy me a cheeseburger, fries and coke on the way home. When Jimmy and Jan took us to the ocean, Erika and Erick, Jan's children, came along so there were five kids. Their nicknames for each other were Brother and Sister. We thought those were their real names so we called them that, too. It was always fun going with Jimmy and Jan as we were able to act like kids and probably wouldn't have been able to go camping, fishing and just be kids otherwise.

Erika and Erick, their children, were a few years younger then I was but we all got along together fine.

At home the spankings became more frequent, and school was our escape. Connie developed a bladder infection and would urinate while playing outside. She'd run into the house and pretty soon she'd come outside and sit on the porch in front of us kids. She'd be crying from a spanking and be wearing her wet underwear on her face. She would just sit there crying with her head down. If she urinated in the house she would get the same spanking and go stand in a corner with her wet underwear on her head. I could see her getting more and more withdrawn with everything Mom was throwing at her.

There was an old abandoned house with long grass and broken windows on McKinley Avenue. Every time we drove by it, Mom pointed and said, "There's Connie's house."

Connie just looked down and didn't say a word, in fear of the wooden spoon. She would do anything for Mom's love and attention, good or bad, but Mom didn't have it in her to give.

Mom did fun things with us as well, like take us three to the drive-in movies. The first movie I remembered seeing was "Planet of the Apes." She would take us about twice a month with a large paper bag of popcorn she popped beforehand. It was also fun to go play on the drive-in's playground before the movie started.

We three kids usually sat in the back seat and I always wanted the middle, that way I could peek between the front seat if a nude part was coming up. Mom would always say,

"Cover your eyes" and I acted like mine were covered. I would look at the partially dressed women until Barbara or Connie told on me.

"Mommy, David is peeking again" and I would get yelled at or get the wooden spoon.

Dad bought Barbara and me new bikes that Christmas, but mine was stolen within two days. New bikes didn't last long in that neighborhood; people would steal anything that looked of value.

Connie got Barbara's old bike. She got all of Barbara's hand-me-down clothes from Goodwill, too. It didn't matter too much about the clothes. We all looked like misfits and welfare kids.

Mom went dancing on the weekends and occasionally there would be a strange man in the house in the morning.

One day she sat us down and said, "You kids are going to have a new brother or sister." I don't recall seeing that guy again after she told us she was pregnant.

My brother Steven was born in 1970. It was a little after Steven was born that we started to see another man who was pretty young-looking come over more and more often.

He called himself Buck.

CHAPTER 4

I'LL BEAT YOU LIKE A STEPCHILD

Buck tricked us kids pretty good at first into liking him. He was twenty- three years old, in the army, and quickly moved in. I don't know what he and Mom were thinking, because there were four of us kids now, none his, and a ten-year difference in age between him and Mom.

I'm guessing Mom was overwhelmed with being a single woman with four kids and thought a man would help her.

I didn't think it would last but before we knew it he gathered us three kids together and said, "Your mom and I are getting married."

He then gave us three a quarter each and we went and bought some candy from the store. We thought that was cool and approved of them getting married. It only cost him seventy five cents to fool us.

Mom said, "You can call him Dad if you want."

I called him "Dad" once but it didn't feel right, and Barbara refused to do it.

A very short time later the major abuse started. When Mom left we got spankings from Buck without knowing why, and often we were locked in the basement until she got home.

Mom always cooked Buck something nice for dinner, and we kids would get a little of what was left or a cheese sandwich, bowl of soup or Hamburger Helper. It was never enough, so, we got our nutrition from school meals.

I joined a softball team and stayed away from home as much as possible. I was in second grade and I rode my bike ten miles to school, then five more miles to softball practice. Then I took my slow, sweet time riding back home the fifteen or so miles.

Our softball team was named "The Roadrunners." We went 21-0, never losing a game. We won the City Championship and I hated to see the season end.

Buck sometimes threw the ball to me outside our home, and if I dropped it he called me dirty names. After a couple of times of practicing with him, I always made excuses not to play catch with him anymore.

I was very proud being on the winning team and was voted Most Improved Player, winning a trophy. Buck later threw my trophy out along with my Roadrunners' baseball cap. I didn't know why. One day after school they were both gone.

We moved several times, and I couldn't even tell you how many different schools we went to.

In third grade I had a crush on a girl in my class. One day we were at recess when the class was called in for a health check. We stood in line and when it was my turn the nurse asked me to take off my shoes and step on the scale. I looked behind me and my girlfriend was there. I didn't want to take off my shoes but the nurse made me. My feet were dirty from the holes in my shoes and I didn't have any socks on.

My girlfriend looked down at my feet and then looked me in the eyes as if she was saying, "Sorry." I was so embarrassed. The nurse looked at me in bewilderment. I stepped on the scale and when she had my weight I just walked away with my head down.

I didn't have socks and neither did Connie. Barbara had two pairs and when I could find a pair of hers I'd wear them, dirty or not. My feet hurt so much! It was a joy to be wearing socks.

This was a hard time for us three kids, moving all the time, not eating, and getting beaten frequently by Buck for no reason. There were times I was so hungry I snuck into the kitchen and ate out of the peanut butter jar with my fingers as fast as I could. When Buck saw finger marks in the peanut butter, off to the bedroom I went and got either the belt or his hand. Connie told me later she used a spoon, but I was so worried about getting caught in the moment that I hurried just to get the peanut butter into my mouth.

Mom and Buck had another couple in their mid-twenties move in with us. The man was in the army with Buck.

The couple hated us kids. They never talked to us, but told on us whenever they could for doing something wrong. They even made up stuff. They slept on the couch and when I was sent to bed in the basement I sometimes snuck up the stairs a little later, after everyone else had gone to bed. I cracked the basement door really slowly and watched the two of them having sex. I'm pretty sure they knew I was watching because the door squeaked while I opened it. I saw her looking at it, pretending not to notice it opening. Then when they finished I hurried to get back into bed, and I heard the door slowly close behind me.

A couple of times when we were the only ones home I came upstairs and she was topless in the living room. She pretended she didn't know I was there and turned to face me. She then let out a little sound as if she was shocked because I was standing there. Still facing me, she slowly put on her bra and shirt. I couldn't understand why she was so evil when others were around, but exposing herself to me when we were alone.

They only lived with us for a few months and when they moved, so did we. It seemed as if every time I made friends at school we moved somewhere else.

I don't recall which school or grade I was in, either third or fourth, but I still chuckle about this today. I used to play marbles with a classmate of mine. His mother let him go home for lunch and one day I went with him. When we walked into his home I stared at his mom's ornament – glass grapes on a vine – which was sitting on the coffee table. There must have been fifteen grapes, and they were exactly the size of big marbles. I talked my friend into cutting about eight of them off, which gave us four apiece. We went back to school and played marbles for the rest of the lunch break.

The next day I asked him if we could go to his house for lunch to get more big marbles. He said, "No, I got whipped and have to stay at school for lunch now!" I was bummed as I had already lost my big marbles playing and needed more.

I have very few memories from those three years, just Buck beating us, going hungry, and Mom turning a blind eye. I don't remember seeing or talking to Dad in this time period. Maybe if he had known what was going on, he would have come and saved us.

We finally moved to a house on 63rd and Portland Avenue in Tacoma, and we stayed there for more than a year.

IS THERE REALLY A GOD? IF SO, PLEASE TAKE US

I started the fifth grade at Boze Elementary in the middle of the school year and had to make all new friends again. I had gone to most of the schools in Tacoma by now and it was taking its toll. By this time I was pretty shy and a bit introverted. I didn't say much in the classroom or at recess, but I used school as an escape from home life.

We moved into a three-bedroom rambler and I shared my room with my brother Steven. It was a modest neighborhood and upscale compared to everywhere else we had lived. I rode my bike around after school with Connie and just kept myself out of the house as much as possible until I was called in.

One day after school I was in the garage working on my bike when I heard a knock on the front door. It was a boy from another class in my school, and I thought, "Cool! He wants to play."

I said, "Hi," and he said, "I'm here to beat you up!"

I was a bit puzzled because I saw him at school and walking home but we had never talked.

I asked, "Why?"

"Because," he said, "I was paid to beat you up."

I looked him over a bit and noticed his long chin. I remembered hearing someone call him "Chin-A-Mar-Rang" one time at school. The nickname fit him well.

I asked, "Where?" and he pointed to a vacant lot across the street. Heck, I wasn't doing anything anyway and I didn't want the other kids at school making fun of me, calling me a "chicken." So we started walking over there.

The whole time walking across the street I was formulating a plan for how to kick his butt. I knew his chin was an easy target and even if I was off a bit with my punches I could still hit him.

We faced each other almost as if we were in a gun fight. Chin-A-Mar-Rang said, "Ready," and we positioned ourselves to have a punch-out.

Chin-A-Mar-Rang threw the first punch and it landed on my chest. Then I threw a punch and connected with his chin. We stood there for about thirty seconds. Then we charged each other. We wrestled for a few minutes, not hurting each other, and we both soon tired out.

We broke our grasp on each other and stood up as if to go at it again after we caught our breath. Then Chin-A-Mar-Rang said, "You want to go play?"

I asked his name and he said, "Jim Rogers."

I said, "Sure."

Jim lived about half a block away and we spent the rest of the afternoon playing. We became inseparable after that and best friends. I later found out that it was Connie who had paid him a quarter to beat me up. I used to pick on Connie quite a bit and she grew tired of it.

Jim was usually a captain on a soccer or tackle football team, and he always picked me first after that for his team during recess. This helped me overcome my shyness a bit because now I was becoming popular with the other kids. Life was starting to change for the better in school anyway.

When we got home from school and Buck was there from work we all had chores. They were to be done perfectly or else…

One day when we three got home from school, Buck told us to follow him. He led us into the backyard, where he opened the crawl-space entrance.

Buck said, "Get under there."

We didn't know what we had done this time. But we knew we had to obey him or get a beating.

We stayed in the one and a half-foot-high, dirt-floor crawl space for what seemed like hours, until he finally came and let us out. I still don't know what half the beatings and putting us into the crawl space was about.

The beatings, at least once a week, were brutal. Most of the time for those Buck would come up with a minor excuse, such as a lint ball under one of our beds, and all three of us would get it.

Usually he used a belt. He stood there with a smirk on his face and said, "Drop your pants and lay over the bed."

A few times he made us watch one another get beaten. I felt sorry for my sisters. I could see the embarrassment on their faces as they lay over the edge of the bed. There was nothing I could do but take the beatings and sometimes watch my sisters take theirs.

I am not sure about my sisters, but there were times when I was hit with a tree branch, and a couple of times a two-by-four.

Buck beat us until we started crying and screaming, so after a few lashes we learned to scream and cry as soon as possible. We didn't talk much about the beatings afterwards because we were separated in different rooms until we stopped crying. Eventually I stopped crying and just let Buck beat me until his arm got tired.

After the beatings we came out of the room and walked by Mom, who wouldn't make eye contact with us. I thought, "Why didn't you stop him?"

We were told never to tell anyone or else, so we kept our mouths shut about it for quite a while.

I later learned that our Mother was also in fear of Buck.

Every Sunday a bus came within a block of our house to pick us up and take us to Sunday school. Almost every Sunday during Mass I ran up to the front of the church to get my piece of cracker and grape juice to "cleanse" myself. I put the cracker in my mouth, drank the grape juice, looked up at the Jesus statue and prayed for Him to take me and my sisters.

One day the three of us were walking from the church bus back home when Barbara pointed towards the sky and said, "Look." We all stopped and stared. There above us was a perfect cloud formation. We could see a lot of steps leading upwards into a building that looked like the front of a beautiful church or temple. On each side at the bottom of the steps was an angel just like those in pictures in the Bible. The stairs seemed to go into the heavens and there were souls in the form of people walking up them.

We stared at the cloud formation for a long time and didn't move or talk. There were barely any other clouds in the sky and it was very clear that it was a message for us kids.

I'm not sure why or how it went away. Maybe we started walking again or the clouds started breaking up, but I remember it vividly.

It was about this time that Mom became pregnant and we had a little brother named Lloyd. He and Steven were the only concern of Mom and Buck. We three felt like orphans sometimes and very much unwanted. I thought a lot about running away to Dad's, but he seldom contacted us. He must have been busy working in the Air Force, and by now he was also taking care of his new girlfriend, Becky, and her two children. I know he loved us, but two tours in Vietnam had changed him. He wasn't the same when he came back.

By now Buck had pretty much isolated us from our grandmother and other family, as most abusers do. The beatings continued as always, and there wasn't anyone to tell to get us out of there.

One day right before summer break – which I dreaded because school was my escape – Buck came home with a friend and said, "She's spending the night." I didn't care. I thought it would have no effect on me.

Or so I thought.

I went to bed and then Mom came in and said, "She will be sleeping in Steven's bed tonight. Steven will sleep on the couch."

I just went to sleep like normal.

I woke up when I heard the bedroom door close and Buck's friend climb into Steven's bed. I drifted back to sleep, but woke up again, feeling the blankets slowly being pulled down from me. I was only ten and didn't know what was going on so I just lay there still. I clenched my eyes shut as she had me lie flat on my back. Then I felt her pulling my underwear down and taking me in her mouth. I was so scared I pretended I was asleep, not knowing what to do.

It was about five minutes later that I was aware of a funny feeling starting to happen. I didn't know what was going on but it began to feel really good, and then my body started shaking and I had a great feeling.

Buck's friend knew that I had had an orgasm. She stood up, pulled my underwear up and tucked the blankets up around me. Not saying a word, she went to bed and I fell asleep.

I woke up and pretended it didn't happen. I only told Barbara.

She said, "No way! You're lying!" So I didn't tell anyone else for many years.

When I came home from school the next day and was told that Buck's friend was spending the night again, I could hardly wait for bedtime. That night I even went to bed early and waited until she came into the bedroom and closed the door. Again she crawled into Steven's bed. This time I lay there pretending to be asleep, waiting for her. After a little bit I felt the covers lowering, and this time she could tell I liked it from looking at my penis. She then took my hand, placing it on her breast, whispering for me to squeeze them until she finished. Then again she tucked me into bed and kissed me on my forehead.

I went to school the next morning and never saw her again. I was kind of depressed when I came home from school and found out she wasn't spending the night. I'm pretty sure Buck knew what had happened by the way he looked at me in the mornings as if to say, "Don't say a word!"

Buck, indirectly or directly, took my innocence. I was never the same little ten-year-old boy again. I doubt Mom knew, but she went along with everything Buck said. It really changed my life from then on. I didn't look at girls in school the same way anymore.

Jim and I had built a clubhouse out of scrap wood in the vacant lot across the street and I took down the "No Girls Allowed" sign. I did everything I could to get Terri, a girl from school, into my clubhouse, but thankfully she always said, "No."

The summer break came and Jim and I spent most of it just playing around the neighborhood. He did have a sister, Laura, one year younger than I, who caught my attention, but I pretty much left her alone until later. We three did go berry picking that summer for about a month. Most of the time Connie and I just had berry fights, so we only made around fifty dollars at the end of the season, but Barbara worked really hard and made lots more. The day we got paid at the end of the season we ran home and showed Mom.

She took it from us, saying, "Now I can buy you school clothes."

It was just like the paper route Barbara and I had. Barbara kept the route money in her dresser drawer. Every month money vanished; Mom and Buck left only enough to pay the bill. We quit after a couple of months because we never had even a penny for our month's work. I could hardly wait for school to start again.

CHAPTER 6

DON'T EVER HIT MY SISTER AGAIN!

The first day of school I found out that Jim was in my class. We both walked around proudly because we were now seniors in the elementary school. Barbara had gone on to Junior High and Connie was in fifth grade.

Connie was in a classroom and, to my surprise, Terri was in her class. Terri, who had long brown hair, freckles and a pretty smile, was a year younger than I, but after my experience with Buck's friend I looked at her differently. When I was in sixth grade I gave her notes on the playground: "Do you like me? Check one, Yes or No." She always wrote back, "Yes, as friends."

I would go to Kmart and buy rings for Terri from the gumball machines for ten cents, hoping I'd see her wearing them the next day. She did a few times for a day or so, but I think she was being nice or they turned her finger green.

I played tag with her and I tried to show off when I knew she was watching us guys play "smear the queer." I looked for her at recess and attempted to do anything that would impress her.

I had a pretty relaxed teacher, Mr. Kelly, who didn't mind if we got up for breaks now and then and left the classroom. I sometimes got up during the day and walked in front of the classroom Terri was in so that maybe she would notice me. One time I even carved a heart with our names on it into the wooden fence at her house. I blew it, though, when instead of trying to impress her with playing sports I started lifting up her skirt and trying to get her into my fort. I had had sexual experience at eleven and Terri, at ten, hadn't, but I sure wanted to teach her. I didn't like the way I was acting towards her, but I thought that if I could show her that feeling of sex she would love me forever.

I'm not sure if I had matured enough or I was just tired of the abuse, but two weeks into the sixth grade I went to the principal.

The humiliation a few days earlier was the turning point.

Buck found one of our beds not made up correctly, so that he couldn't bounce a dime off of it. When Connie and I came home from school we were told to sit on the couch until Barbara returned. When she walked in, Buck and Mom told us to go to our rooms and undress completely. We looked at each other and slowly walked to our rooms. I took my clothes off and sat on the bed, waiting for whatever was coming.

Then Mom came into my room with a towel and a couple of safety pins. She told me to lie on the bed, because she was going to put a diaper on me. She used the towel to make a diaper, put it on me and then told me to wait on my bed.

About five minutes later Buck opened my door and told me to go get into the car. I walked down the hallway with Barbara and Connie in front of me. I was completely naked except for the diaper. Buck and Mom allowed Barbara and Connie to wear a bit of clothing that barely covered their breasts.

We three got in the back seat and Buck, Mom, Loyd and Steven got in the front.

Buck said, "We're going for a ride."

Barbara had tears in her eyes and her arms around her chest, trying to expose as little as possible.

Buck drove us to a corner grocery store one mile from home. Pulling into the parking lot, he turned and handed us each a dime. He smiled and said, "Go buy yourselves a candy bar."

Barbara and Connie took their dimes and slowly left the car. I refused to take mine and said, "No!"

Buck screamed, "Get out of the car!"

I still refused and Buck got out. I thought, *Mom, when are you going to stop this?*

Buck took off his belt and beat me with it until I finally crawled out.

We ran into the grocery store and everyone near the cash register stared at us as we passed by them. We didn't care what candy bars we grabbed, just the ones that were close to the beginning of the aisle. The clerk just stared at us along with everyone else in the store.

I didn't stand in line. I just threw the dime at the clerk and ran out. Why nobody did anything, like call the police or just keep us there for some kind of child abuse worker to find out what was going on, is beyond me. Perhaps they were in shock and didn't know what to do.

When we went outside, Buck and Mom had driven away and left us there to walk home. We tried our best to get home without anybody seeing us but it was impossible.

Whenever a car drove by, Barbara ran behind bushes. Then, when there were no cars coming, she sprinted to the next bush.

We had to go past our school and a few of my friends saw me running by. I really didn't want to go to school the next day because I was sure everyone would hear about it. To my surprise the few who had seen me didn't say anything. They felt sorry for me. Those eleven-year-olds could keep a secret. But the principal wouldn't.

We finally made it home and were told to go put our clothes back on and clean our rooms.

That's when I noticed my comic book collection gone. I collected comic books, like most kids then, and was very proud of them.

I asked Mom, "Where is my comic book collection?"

She said, "Buck burned them in the fireplace."

I decided then that I wasn't going to let this abuse happen any longer. I got up the courage to go to the principal's office and tell him everything.

He looked at me and said, "I'll look into this."

I felt very good for the rest of the school day. Finally someone was going to help us! It was as if a big weight had been lifted off my shoulders. I didn't have to watch my sisters being beaten anymore, wearing diapers and or being put under the house. I had finally mustered up enough hatred towards Buck and Mom that I had talked.

I walked home from school, opened the front door, and was grabbed by the hair. My principal had looked into it, alright. The only thing he did was call Mom and ask, "Is this happening?"

She said, "No," and that was the end of his investigation.

Buck led me into my bedroom and beat me until I didn't feel it anymore. I kept hearing him saying over and over again, "I told you not to tell anyone."

When he was through, I got up from the bed and stared right into his eyes with deep hatred. I was done letting Buck see me cry. He slapped me across my face, knocking me to the floor. I stood up again, and he knocked me to the floor again. I wasn't going to cry.

He stormed out of my room, slamming the door behind him.

It was about fifteen minutes later. All three of us were told to go to the backyard. We walked out back and were shoved under the house. I sat there in that dark, dirty hole looking at Connie and Barbara and said, "Screw this!" Lying on my side, I began kicking at the wood frame of the crawl-space door.

I kicked with all my might. After a few whacks the frame started to break. I looked at my sisters and said, "We're getting out of here right now."

Connie pleaded for me to stop, but I kept on kicking at the frame. I'm not sure if it was a coincidence, but as soon as the frame snapped and went outwards, Buck lowered his face with perfect timing.

The wood from the broken frame slapped Buck right across his face.

After that we were grounded to our rooms for a week, except for school. The beatings did slow, but we got the silent treatment.

After our week of grounding, Mom told us to come out of our rooms and sit in the living room.

I had been selling Christmas cards during the Christmas season, three months earlier. There were about five boxes left over that I hadn't been able to have people purchase. Mom told us to get our coats on and go sell the Christmas cards.

She said, "You're not going to eat unless you sell them."

Buck usually spent the food money on his car, and food was a third or fourth priority for us three kids. Buck and Mom were having frequent arguments and he left with all the money. We had to sell the cards because there was no food and no way to get any.

However, it was mid-March, dark and raining, and it was going to be pretty tough. We went out for a few hours trying to sell our cards, but nobody would buy them. They would just stare at us with a puzzled look or laugh and close their door. We returned home soaking wet and went to our rooms hungry. We were fortunate that our schools served breakfast and lunch. We learned to go over to friends' houses and eat there if they would let us.

Jim's grandmother, Beverly, made me a sandwich or something else to eat when I went there after school, which was almost daily. Beverly, smiling, would hand me a sandwich and usually a treat. I could only spend a few minutes there but I ate on the way home.

Buck knew that he couldn't intimidate me anymore. I was only eleven, but he couldn't beat me enough to feel like the punk that he was, so he used beating Barbara and Connie against me.

The last straw for me came one day when I was working on my bicycle in the garage and had it half torn apart, greasing the bearings. Connie came out and we started talking about school. Then I saw the garage door open from the dining room and Buck come out charging with a dustpan in his hand. On the dustpan I could see a lint ball about the size of a dime.

Buck started screaming at Connie, and then pushed her with all his might across the garage.

I yelled, "Don't you ever touch my sister again!" At the same time I reached for my bicycle chain, picked it up and hit Buck across the face with it.

Buck's face opened up. Furious, he beat the crap out of me. However, I had let him know, "Do not touch my sisters again!"

About a week later we three kids were called into the living room once more.

Mom said, "I talked with your dad. You three are going to go live with him in Hawaii. I'm going to sell everything you have, and in four days I'll take you to the airport."

I didn't see Buck again, but I always swore I was coming after him when I got big enough. That didn't happen, though, because his bad karma got him first.

I said goodbye to my friends and was kind of sad leaving them, but it was better than staying in the situation we were in. Jim and I made a pact that we wouldn't lose touch but would write.

Jim said, "Let's be bloodbrothers."

We cut our thumbs so they would bleed and then we put our thumbs together. Jim wanted to cut our wrists but neither of us could do it. So now we were bloodbrothers for life and nothing could separate us.

We talked about Hawaii for a little while and Jim brought up a very interesting question: "Do you think them dancers wearing them grass skirts wear underwear?"

I didn't know but I sure wanted to find out, promising I would let him know when I knew. Then I asked him to tell Terri goodbye for me and left.

Mom drove us to the airport and hugged Barbara and Connie goodbye. I pulled away from her, not wanting a hug, I just wanted out of there before she changed her mind. Barbara and Connie cried, but I got on the plane and waited anxiously for a pretty Hawaiian woman to put a lei around my neck and say, "Welcome to Hawaii."

CHAPTER 7

HAWAII, WE'RE SAVED!

When the plane touched down on the ground on the island of Oahu I looked at Barbara and Connie and both of them had an expression on their faces as if to ask, "What now?" Taking the lead I ran off the plane, leaving my sisters behind me. When I reached the arrivals area, I was disappointed when I didn't see a pretty Hawaiian woman there.

Instead, I saw Dad, Becky and her two daughters. I stopped in my tracks.

Becky was the first to approach me.

"Hi, David," she said. "Welcome to Hawaii."

She kissed me on my cheek and placed a lei around my neck. Dad picked me up and gave me a big hug, then introduced me to my two step-sisters, Kim and Cheri. It went the same way for Barbara and Connie when they arrived, and all three of us had smiles on our faces the whole time. It was the first time we felt like smiling in a long time; it felt good.

We went to pick up our suitcases and, on the way, Dad took off our coats and tossed them into the trash can, saying, "You don't have to wear clothes like this anymore."

When we got our bags he went over to the seats, opened them up and went through them for a few minutes. Then he took all three of them and dumped them into the garbage can.

He turned and said, "Let's go to the mall. These kids need clothes."

The three of us looked at each other with big smiles and we each knew what the others were thinking. The mall, not the Goodwill!

We all got into the Chevy Impala convertible and headed toward the mall. My eyes were as big as saucers. It was as if a dream had come true, the warm wind hitting my face, feeling as if someone finally cared about me and my sisters. We drove by a few sights and Becky sounded excited as she told us about the buildings and the beaches as if she was a tour guide.

When we got to the mall, Dad took my hand and said to the others, "You girls go together, get what you want, and David and I will meet you in an hour or so at the food court."

Dad and I took off to the boys' clothes section and he said, "Start picking out some clothes."

Then he stopped, grabbed a Shakey's Pizza Parlor shirt and a pair of jeans, and took me to the changing room.

He said, "Put these on and leave the clothes you're wearing in the garbage can."

I did and soon we were picking out clothes. He had told me, "Get what you want," and I was nervous, so I'd grab one pair of pants, try them on and if they fit he'd say, "Get two more pairs if you like them."

After I got new underwear, socks, pants and shirts, Dad took my hand and we went to the shoe department. I stared at some tennis shoes that I had always wanted but only dreamed about. Dad could tell I wanted them but was too nervous to ask. The salesclerk came up, and Dad told her to fit me with a pair of those tennis shoes. They cost over twenty dollars. I was in shock that Dad would pay that much for a pair of shoes for me, but he did.

We made our way to the food court where I saw the girls sitting around a table, eating and laughing. I was so proud of what I was wearing I strutted up to them, (as much as an eleven-year-old could), and looked at them.

Barbara and Connie had so much more life in them, it was if they had been re-born. I got a bit jealous when they didn't offer me any of their hot dogs, because we always shared so no one went hungry.

When Dad asked, "David, you hungry?" I almost fell out of my chair. He handed me a ten and said, "Go get something to eat. You need to put some weight on."

I ordered a couple of hot dogs, nachos and a slushie and pigged out. It felt weird being able to eat all I wanted and not having to share with Barbara and Connie.

When I finished we all loaded back into the car and headed to our new home.

When we got to the apartment we ran inside to check it out. There was new furniture, food in the cabinets and a bed where the kitchen table should be.

Dad said, "I didn't have time to get a bigger place, so for now you sleep here and the four girls get the second bedroom."

I didn't care. I was just happy to be there.

Becky told us kids to go walk around the complex and check it out, so we all took off. We went to the swimming pool and even met some new friends on the way. One girl who was about Barbara's age, thirteen or so, had a halter top on and I immediately noticed her breasts. She wasn't wearing a bra!

We ran around the complex for a couple of hours just having fun and then went back for dinner. As we all sat around the TV eating, I thought, *Wow! There's plenty of steak on all our plates.*

Dad said, "Eat up, boy. Put some meat on them bones."

I finished and then I went to lie on my bed in the dining room because I was exhausted.

I was awakened around eight o'clock the next morning by Kim and Cheri when they turned on the cartoons, and the rest of the family slowly got up. Becky showed us where the cereal was and we all filled our own bowls. They had Cap'n Crunch's Peanut Butter, so I ate two bowls because it was good and I had never eaten it before.

We actually were asked to sit around the table and have a family discussion. The first thought I had was, *okay, someone's going to get a spanking. What did we do now?*

Dad was dressed in his uniform to go to work at the Air Force Base, and he asked us if we wanted to take a week off school or start the next day. It wasn't hard to decide. We all voted on next week.

So we played for a week around the complex, swam, even ventured out a bit into the surrounding apartments, exploring and making new friends.

Dad took one of those days off and he and I went to Waikiki for the day. My hair was buzzed off, so Dad went into a gift shop and bought me a baseball cap.

"Put this on your head, boy, or you're going to burn," he said laughing. I was pure white coming from Washington State and I did get some color that day.

I was just about to turn twelve and, because of my sexual experience, all I could do that day was stare at all the beautiful girls and women in their bikinis. Women were lying all over the beach. Every once in a while I walked around and got a close-up look as they tanned. I stared mostly at the ones who had unfastened their tops so they wouldn't get tan lines, just hoping they would lean over and expose some breast.

Then it happened. Dad said, "See the woman over there with her top unfastened?"

I said, "Yes."

He said, "I'll give you a buck if you take this ice cube and put it on her back."

I knew the reason for doing this and I wanted her to jump up too so I could see her breasts. I took the buck and the ice cube and went on my mission to get her to get up quickly. Hopefully she would forget her top was unfastened.

I slowly walked towards her as her head was turned away from me and placed the ice cube on her back. She jumped up just enough that I got to see her breasts. Quite a few other people did too. She started yelling at me in front of all the people there on the beach. I walked back to Dad with my head down but excited that I got to see my first breasts in Hawaii.

Buck had turned me into an animal; I wanted to see more of the female body and have another sexual experience.

We packed up right after that and I was sworn to secrecy from telling Becky. I don't think Dad really cared if Becky knew or not though; one time later on he had me do it in front of her.

I felt as if I was dreaming and it would all end soon.

During the first month or so I had trouble believing that I really deserved this much fun without getting in trouble. When the family went shopping, to the beach or sightseeing, I'd say, "I don't want to go."

They would try to get me to go with them but I refused and they went without me. Then I'd write a note to them saying I had run away and they would never find me. I'd leave it on the coffee table and hide under the sink or in the closet waiting for them to come home and read it.

I usually picked up the note and went off to play before they came home, but one time I didn't. They read the note and found me in the closet. Dad knew I was needing attention, and from then on they never let me stay home while they went anywhere again. He also wanted me to go see a psychiatrist but I refused, and eventually he dropped it.

My sisters and I went to school, which finished three weeks later; then it was summer break. Becky and Dad worked so we kids pretty much had the apartment to ourselves during the day. Connie and I went around during the day knocking on doors collecting pop bottles and got a few bucks in our pockets. Barbara washed taxi cabs and worked most of the summer. Connie also did odd jobs for people but she was always trying to figure out how to make more money.

Connie wanted a quarter for a candy bar and I made a deal with her. I made up a water balloon and told her if she could catch it without it breaking I'd give it to her. One catch though – there was a thirteen-story apartment building on the other side of our parking lot. I went to the top floor and climbed over the fence, while Connie waited below.

Then I dropped the water balloon, giving it a little emphasis.

Connie actually tried to catch it, almost taking her forearm off. The water balloon broke, of course, and I never gave her the quarter.

Connie's forearm was bruised for a couple of weeks, and did I ever get yelled at for that one! I lost my two dollar allowance for the week; Dad gave it to Connie.

Barbara, being a couple of years older, wouldn't fall for my antics. But Barbara had older girlfriends with breasts.

One afternoon she had one of her girlfriends over. I really wanted to lift her halter top up and see her breasts. When Barbara went to the bathroom, I had my chance. As soon as she closed the door I walked up to her girlfriend and lifted her top. I startled her, so I got a good look for a few seconds before she could pull her top back down. She never told Barbara or I would have heard about it from Dad or Becky.

A week later Barbara's friend came over again and she was wearing a halter top. Barbara went into the kitchen to make lunch; it was just us two alone together.

Barbara's friend noticed that I was staring at her chest, and to my surprise she lifted her top.

Then she got up, giggling, walked over to me and said, "You want to touch them?"

I had my hands on her breasts really fast; she let me massage them for a minute or so. Then she went into the kitchen. I think Barbara knew something was up because after that, every time the friend came around, they went directly into Barbara's bedroom keeping me away from her.

One time, though, I was walking past the outdoor swimming pool when I saw Barbara's friend in there swimming. Darn! I ran to the apartment, put on my swim trunks and headed for the pool. I jumped in and stood in the shallow side up to my neck. She kept swimming around me, giggling and flirting with me. When nobody was looking (at least we didn't think anyone was looking), she swam to me, stopped in front of me and we started talking. Her hand grabbed my crotch and, when I didn't protest, she put her hand down my trunks. My hand went right for her bikini bottoms, trying to lower them. She stopped me and slid my hand down her bottoms. I fell instantly in lust with her, but she avoided me after that and we didn't see each other again.

One day Dad sat us three down and told us Mom had called. Dad told us,

"Your mom wants you to go back and live with her, so you three need to talk about this."

He left for his bedroom and we heard him crying in his room.

We three quickly decided to stay with Dad and Barbara went and told him our decision to stay. He came out of his room and gave us three big hugs saying,

"I love you!" and I knew he meant it.

I turned twelve that summer and all I could think about was having sex.

In the seventh grade I didn't really fit in. If a girl talked to me I always said something sexual, and the girls weren't ready for that yet. I felt cheated that I had lost my innocence at such a young age and felt different from my friends.

In October we all sat around the couch and Dad said, "I'm up for a promotion so we might have to move. Let's vote."

Everyone was ready to go back to the mainland except Barbara. Barbara loved living in Hawaii but was outvoted.

We started packing about a month later and learned we were moving to Columbus, Ohio.

Becky, Kim and Cheri left two weeks before the rest of us to find a place to live so that when we got there we could all just settle in. We three kids and Dad stayed at a hotel on the beach before leaving. Dad gave us money each morning and told us to meet him somewhere for lunch or dinner, leaving us to roam.

One day at lunch he handed us three tickets to go see the Polynesian women dance. My first thought, of course, was, *I wonder if they wear panties?*

We went to the show and I stood as close as I could get. As the women started dancing, I stared as hard as I could to catch a peek up their grass skirts. Darn it, it was either too dark or they wore black panties.

I wrote to Jim the next day and told him, "Dude, they don't wear panties. I saw all of it."

I also sent him a picture of me at the beach with the bluest ocean water in the background.

We three also went on the Pearl Harbor Cruise, ran around the beach, and had a blast. We boarded the cruise boat at a run. It was going to be a nice cruise on a nice boat that carried 50 people comfortably.

We cruised around the Island for a little while and then headed for Pearl Harbor. I saw the Arizona Memorial and part of the ship still sticking out of the water, with oil bubbling up around it occasionally causing a light sheen on the water.

We were given a booklet describing what had happened on December 7, 1941. It told the story of how many sailors lost their lives that day and had some photographs of the real attack. I cherished that booklet for the longest time until I lost it many years later.

When the tour was over I started to look for Barbara and Connie. I searched everywhere for about ten minutes, but couldn't find them, and I began to think they had fallen overboard.

Finally I found a crew member and said, "My sisters fell overboard. Stop the ship."

The crew member smiled and grabbed my hand.

"Come with me," she said. "I'll show you where they are."

She took me to the galley and said, "There they are, under that table." Then she left.

I looked under the table and saw Barbara and Connie cuddled together. They looked green and were as sick as you can imagine. I couldn't help myself; I started laughing as I tried to help them out from under the table. They were having no part of that until the boat docked.

For many years afterwards I joked with my sisters about getting seasick. I've never seen two girls pushing their way off a boat like that before. Nobody could stand in their way. We had to head back to the hotel so they could lie down for a while. I helped them into our room, lay them down and took off downstairs.

One thing that still haunts me is that I was walking by a pinball machine by myself when I spotted a change purse. I grabbed it and took it to my room. Inside I found a woman's watch and about thirty dollars in cash. The watch was a very nice one with diamonds and gold facing. I knew it was expensive, probably a wedding present of value.

I didn't turn it in. Instead I headed back to the pinball machines. While I was walking towards them I saw a couple in their mid-twenties standing there and the woman was crying. I knew why. I had her watch.

I hesitated for a minute or so, deciding what to do. I made the wrong choice – I turned and walked away. I regret it deeply to this day and I wish I could take back that moment in time, I would make a different choice.

I walked down the beach where I noticed Dad lying down with a woman rubbing oil on his back. Being young and dumb I went up to them. I got such a dirty look from my dad that I knew I had just walked into something I shouldn't have. She was pleasant and even rubbed oil on my back.

Dad got up after a little while and I saw them going to our hotel holding hands. He had his own room and she was staying with him. I was told to keep my mouth shut or else, so I did.

I had the second key to Dad's room, and I walked in one morning. I could hear them in the shower. I peeked around the corner and watched them being intimate through the glass doors.

Everything Dad did revolved around women, and if he could have sex with them he did.

When we were off on our own, whenever he saw a nice looking woman he asked, "How would you like to get her in bed?"

I wanted to make Dad feel proud of me so I always answered, "Yes."

I knew the concept of how to have sex but didn't really understand it yet. Dad was bound and determined to get me thinking about it as often as he did.

We boarded the plane back to the mainland and landed in Columbus, Ohio.

CHAPTER 8

PACK UP, WE'RE MOVING TO OHIO

On the various planes heading to Ohio, Dad flirted with all the stewardesses. Sometimes it was a little embarrassing. When we landed in Columbus, Becky met us. She walked up and hugged Dad, then she hugged us three kids and I looked down her shirt as she bent over to give me my hug. I thought, *She doesn't know my dad was with another woman.* I also noticed that she had the same body type as the woman who I saw being intimate with Dad in the shower.

Becky was about ten years younger than Dad. She was slim and had a really nice figure, and she was nice to me. I began to look differently towards her. Becky was no longer my step-mom; Becky was a woman. I started thinking at that moment, *If he can have sex with other women, then I want to be intimate with Becky.* I now realized that Becky was a woman with experience, and I wanted her to be my teacher.

We got into a rental car and headed to the hotel we were going to stay at until we found a house to rent. The hotel was nicely furnished, and we enjoyed it as we waited for our stuff to arrive from Hawaii.

We didn't have winter clothes and, it being October in Ohio, it was cold. Dad asked me what kind of coat I wanted and I told him a Cleveland Browns coat. A couple of days later he came home with a Cincinnati Bengals coat and I just about died.

"Dad, everyone likes the Cleveland Browns here."

He offered to take it back, but I liked the orange and black colors so I decided to keep it.

We got a house, moved into it and I started school. I wore my Cincinnati Bengals coat and the very first day the kids started making fun of me. I thought about throwing it away but decided to stand my ground and wear it. I must have been in five fights defending my Bengals before they finally backed off. Still today my team is the Cincinnati Bengals. Go Bengals! That was actually a great turning point in my life because I learned to stick up for myself.

We had a four-bedroom house so I got my own room. I started a paper route right away and made some pocket money. Connie and I also went through the neighborhood cutting grass in the summer and shovel snow in the winter. Connie always asked for money, so I would give her two dollars to deliver the papers that day. Life was good, Connie delivering my newspapers and me kicking back. Connie did my paper route and I bought sports memorabilia with all the extra cash.

I had a nice collection of postcards from Hawaii in a photo album. I brought a friend home from school one day and grabbed the photo album to show it off. It was a pretty good collection with about fifty cards: mountains, beaches, the volcano, pineapple fields and much more. I went through them slowly, telling him all about what I had seen there.

On the last page I had my most prized postcard: one with the picture of a Hawaiian woman on the beach with only a bikini bottom on. I finally got to the last page, turned the page over and – it was gone! I started flipping through the pages, hoping I had missed it, but no, it was gone. I searched all my dresser drawers, under the bed, and the whole room and couldn't find it.

I asked Barbara and Connie where it was. "I don't know," they both said.

I went downstairs and Becky was in the kitchen. "Do you know where my postcard of the Hawaiian woman with no top on is?" I asked.

Becky turned and said with a smile, "I don't know."

I could tell right away she had taken it. I was devastated. My Hawaiian woman was gone forever.

I also started collecting baseball cards and had quite a collection of the "Big Red Machine," the 1975 Cincinnati Reds. I turned my room into a sports theme: football posters on my wall, baseball caps, baseball comforter and jerseys. I really got into sandlot sports and became quite athletic. Even the boys a few years older than I picked me for their team, as I was very competitive and could hang with them. I wanted to sign up for an organized sport with kids my age but we couldn't afford it.

I had a lot of girls my age chasing me by now, as well as most of Connie's girlfriends.

Connie complained to me a few times saying, "I bring my girlfriends home and they just want to talk to you."

I liked the attention so I let it happen. They all had breasts by now and most were slim and liked to touch my leg or arms while chatting. However, I had my mind on a slim girl in my class who wore black bras with white blouses most of the time. Melinda was her name and I let it be known I liked her.

One day I was doing something in my front yard and Melinda came over to visit. She was wearing pretty short shorts and a t-shirt with no bra. We chatted for a little while, and then she asked if I'd be her boyfriend.

I said, "Yes, if you'll go to the river with me."

It was actually a stream that ran about eight feet across, and you could walk across it. I had a perfect secluded spot in the trees and bushes for privacy. We jumped on my bike and I peddled down there, where we made our way to my secluded area. We kissed for a while as my hands explored her body.

It wasn't long before we were both undressed and looking for a nice spot to lie down, but there was no place we could do this without getting dirty or getting needles on our butts. We argued for a little while about who was going to lie on the ground, and finally Melinda did. I cuddled with her and we began to kiss again.

Then within a couple minutes I heard a horrible sound: "Melinda! Melinda!" It was her dad yelling.

We got dressed quickly and headed out to see what he wanted. When we came out of the bushes, he told her, "*Get in that car!*" and pointed his finger at me saying, "I'm calling your parents!"

I didn't go home for a couple of hours, expecting I would be in trouble. Then I opened the front door slowly so as not to make any noise, walked carefully up the stairs and into my bedroom, and closed the door behind me. About half an hour later, Dad came up, walked into my room and closed the door behind him.

He walked towards me and said, "How far did you get?"

I didn't answer him. He said, "Someday you'll be bringing them home to share with me."

I sat there for a little time, not knowing that he was serious. He smiled at me and I thought, *Oh, my God, I have turned into my dad. All I want to do is have sex!*

Dad said, "Dinner's ready," and then left my room.

The next day at school I asked Melinda what had happened. She told me she was grounded for a month and couldn't talk to me or see me again out of school.

Even our teachers were told; whenever we got together to talk at school they separated us.

At this time Dad started to struggle financially, providing for seven people. I still had my paper route and Becky borrowed money from me from time to time. When I gave it to her, I thought that she might reward me with intimacy.

This was also the first time Dad hit me across the face.

I am not sure what I did, and it wasn't my fault, but I wasn't mature enough to understand his struggles. He started ridiculing me every chance he could. We went fishing one morning with Becky's father and I got yelled at loudly for reeling in too fast. It was only the second or third time I had ever fished so I didn't know how.

Dad started calling me names in front of his friends, the neighbors and my friends. Family life was just out of his comfort zone. He started not coming home at night, arguing with Becky all the time and throwing things. The family was dividing right before our eyes, and although Becky tried to keep it together, there was nothing she could do.

I was next to Dad and Becky's bedroom and I could hear Becky crying at night when Dad didn't come home. I lay there feeling sorry for her, wondering what I could do.

One night Dad told me, "Sex is a cure-all. All women are horny."

I would lie in bed at night fantasizing about Becky.

I started leaving my door cracked open a bit so that when Becky walked by she would see me and hopefully walk in. I also sometimes watched her undress, because her door was hardly ever closed all the way. I would see her slip into her nightgown or just crawl into bed naked.

I kept trying to get up the nerve to go in and make love to her or have her come into my room and satisfy her needs.

Again Dad always told me, "Take it when it is there to take." I began to think Becky was leaving the door open enough for me to watch her because she wanted me to come on in. After all, she would be the last to go to bed. At fourteen I thought nobody would know but us two.

I slept naked. I couldn't understand why Becky passed by instead of coming in every night that Dad wasn't home. After all, I could be the best she had ever had, and she could get even with Dad.

I grew up thinking about women like Dad did.

He told me, "It's just a hole with hair around it." Other than sleeping with women, he said, they were good for housekeeping and cooking.

Dad had all of us sitting around the table one evening, and said, "I'm retiring out of the Air Force." Okay, we didn't know what that exactly meant but whatever you say, Dad.

It wasn't long before Becky ended up with a black eye and I asked, "What happened?"

She answered, "I ran into a door."

I didn't figure out that Dad had hit her until I got punched myself.

Then Dad came up to me, which I avoided as much as possible at that time, and said, "We're moving to California in two days. Don't tell anyone."

So we all started packing, loaded the moving truck and did a very early morning move, leaving all the unpaid bills behind. This time I didn't even get to tell my friends goodbye. We just disappeared. One day we were there and the next day we were gone.

CHAPTER 9

WE'LL MAKE DO
WITHOUT YOU, DAD

We didn't know it but we were making a pit stop in Omaha to visit Dad's brothers, then off to California. Barbara, Connie and I, after a brief meeting with Uncle Al and his family, stayed at their home while Dad, Becky, Kim and Cheri took off for a few days. I'm still not sure where they went, but a couple of days later they came back. We weren't abandoned, but it was strange that they had just disappeared.

Al and his family were very pleasant and made us feel welcomed.

Becky came back first and sat us three down. She asked, "Do you kids want to live in Omaha?"

We all said, "Yes," and she said, "That would make your dad feel really good."

We actually thought Becky and Dad were married, but found out then that they were just living together as boyfriend and girlfriend. It actually turned out to be a very good two years, because I was fourteen now and less shy.

We found a house in a pretty good neighborhood that had enough room for us all. Again I had my own bedroom, and I set it up with my sports memorabilia. We lived on a corner and we had an old wooden building out back that I quickly turned into a clubhouse.

The best thing as far as I was concerned was that two teenagers lived next door – Bill, who was my age, and Melody, who was one year younger than I was.

Dad's brothers, John and Al, came over to help paint the inside of our new home before we moved in. John, Dad's oldest brother, had a son a year younger than I. Danny and I quickly became friends and hung out a lot.

Bill and I played catch at a baseball field a couple of blocks away from our houses. There was also Randy, who was my age and lived cater-cornered to us, so if one boy couldn't play there were others outside. Connie told me that a set of triplets her age lived up the street – two boys and one girl, Joe, John and Jeannie.

I started the ninth grade and was pretty happy about my new beginning. I quickly got a girlfriend, Dolly. She was Randy's cousin and went to my school in the same grade. We walked around school holding hands and rode the school bus home together. A few days into our "going together" I found out she smoked pot. She asked me if I wanted to try it and I said, "No."

I wasn't into cigarettes or pot and decided to drop Dolly. I didn't want to hurt her feelings so Danny and I devised a plan. Danny had a girlfriend he wasn't happy with either, but I thought she was cute. So all four of us got together at my house. Danny and I planned on playing hide and go seek. He would find Dolly and I would find his girlfriend. He would make out with Dolly and I would make out with his girlfriend.

It worked out perfectly and we switched girlfriends that day. I didn't stay with my new girlfriend long, though, because she lived so far away, and Danny soon broke up with Dolly.

I started paying attention to Melody and soon we were going together. We met in my clubhouse at certain times and made out.

Melody was a cute girl and she let it be known she wanted to lose her virginity to me. I took a different route, though: baseball, football, soccer, and track and field. I was becoming quite an athlete and the captain on most teams. I attribute this to Dad at the time; he stayed home and we enjoyed the family life.

The 1976 Olympic summer games made me want to be in really great shape. They inspired me into wanting to be an Olympic athlete. Danny and I started lifting weights, running and just working out.

Melody and I met out back now and then and made out, but my interest in having sex wasn't there anymore. I was going to be an Olympic athlete!

One day that summer I was walking to the corner store when I noticed my sister Connie in a group of people and went to investigate. I walked up to her and before she could put it out I saw her smoking a cigarette. A few of my friends were there, too, Melody, Bill and Randy, as well as a stunning girl with long brown hair.

I didn't say a word about the smoking but I gave Connie a dirty look. While I was talking to everyone, Connie lit up another one and said, "Here. Want to try it?" I looked at the girl with long brown hair and she nodded, "Yes."

I took it out of Connie's hand and began smoking right then and there. It was at that moment my dreams of becoming an Olympic athlete vanished.

I walked Connie and the brown-haired girl back to our house and Connie said, "You can't tell Dad because you smoked, too."

She was right, I couldn't say a word.

I didn't care about the cigarette smoking. I had this girl on my mind.

I asked Connie after she left, "Who is she?" and Connie answered, "Jeannie."

An aura of perfection surrounded Jeannie. She had a beautiful smile, freckles and just enough shyness to make her adorable. I broke up with Melody and made it well known I liked Jeannie. It took a couple of weeks but soon Jeannie and I were boyfriend and girlfriend. Her parents were very protective of her and we had to hide our relationship from them.

I knew Jeannie was a virgin so we would mainly just kiss and hold hands. I didn't want to destroy her perfection so I didn't go there. I learned at this time that females were not only "holes with hair around them" but much more.

One day I learned something from one of her brothers, that she wanted me to take her virginity.

I was fifteen now and Jeannie was fourteen and I thought, *Why not? We're going to be together forever.*

A couple of days later, when Jeannie's parents were at work, eight of us were in her basement. We decided to play Truth or Dare. We gathered in a circle and took turns spinning a bottle around on the floor. When the bottle stopped in front of one of us, we asked that person a question, or the person could take a dare, not knowing what it was.

We played for a little while and I spun the bottle and got it to stop while pointing towards Jeannie.

I asked Jeannie, "Truth or dare?"

Jeannie answered, "Dare."

I said, "I dare you to take me upstairs, take off your clothes and get in bed with me."

As our friends cheered her on, she grabbed my hand and we went up to her bedroom.

We undressed in front of each other and stood there naked. Jeannie's body was perfect. I just stared at her and she stared at me. Then she crawled into her bed and we got under the sheets together. We petted for a while and then there was a knock on her door.

Her brother Joe said through the door, "Dave, don't get her pregnant."

Jeannie lay there like an angel, urging me to get on top of her. I did and we kissed passionately until I knew it was time.

I wanted to stare into her eyes as I turned her into a woman. We parted our lips and looked deep into each other's eyes.

Jeannie whispered, "Please," and I said, "No, not yet."

I couldn't do it; I didn't want to destroy her perfection.

She had a stunned, hurt expression on her face. I told her as we were getting dressed, "I love you," and she replied, "I love you, too." We kissed and went back to the basement.

As far as everyone knew we had gone through with it. Jeannie wanted everyone to think we did so I went along with her.

It was only a couple of weeks after that that I learned Jeannie and her family were moving to another state. I was devastated for quite a while. I had lost the love of my life. I did have a lot of pride in myself though, because I was not going to be the one to destroy perfection.

I went back with Melody off and on but never tried to get into her pants. She tried hard for us to become intimate, but the feelings just weren't there for me.

Becky and Dad were both working so there was plenty of food and extra spending money. Dad was selling life insurance and Becky worked at a hospital.

Dad was also a very good car mechanic and body repairman. During the summer of 1977 he bought a 1969 Granada for Barbara. He spent most of his weekends fixing it up and gave it to her for school. Dad would work all weekends on that car and if he wasn't working on it, he was working on something else. I remember he was always busy helping others or doing something for us kids. Connie and I also worked our first jobs that summer detassling corn. That job was the worst I ever had. We were bused out of Omaha into the cornfields along with about thirty other teenagers. We would get to the cornfields around sunup and all slowly get off the bus. Then we would all line up in front of a different row of cornstalks and go through picking the flowery part off of the top.

By ten AM or so it was so hot that we'd be drinking as much water as we could. We had to wear pants and longsleeved shirts so the leaves of the cornstalks wouldn't cut our arms or legs. The first day most of the girls wore shorts and by the end of the day their legs were all scratched. The second day everyone was wearing pants and longsleeve-shirts. They also irrigated early morning so the dirt turned into mud and you'd sink down into it. Most of us wore boots so you could pull your feet out of the mud without losing your shoes. We would usually have to quit for the day in the early afternoon as most of the time it was over 100 degrees. We worked for about six weeks until the season ended. I started the tenth grade that year and now was in high school.

Life was good as I was doing well in school and had extra spending money. I would help Dad on the weekends sometimes and he would pay me pretty well. I also had my learner's permit and occasionally Becky would let me drive Barbara's car. Dad was really trying to be a family man and then it happened, Dad started seeing another woman named Helen.

Dad started not coming home at night again and soon there was barely any food in the house. He only came home a few times, on Becky's pleading. Becky wanted him back and made up a very nice dinner when she knew he'd be home. She set up the table really nicely and we all sat down for dinner.

By this time we three would only talk to him when he spoke to us. He was a ticking timebomb and nobody wanted to say the wrong thing. We could tell he didn't want to be there and a lot of times I didn't want him there, either.

Several times when we sat down for dinner Becky fixed Dad's plate. He would look at it, grab it and throw it across the room. Then he would say, "I'm not eating this crap," and storm out of the house.

When he did stay for dinner and spend the night, I'd see Becky the next morning and a few times she was sporting a black eye.

He usually didn't come home for several days or weeks and everyone just waited for the next time he returned. Hearing Becky crying in her bedroom, I felt so sorry for her and I wanted to make her feel better. This made me start thinking again about how much I wanted her.

We moved into another house, one with an open basement. There was a bedroom down there and a shower. The basement was split in half with a wall between the shower and the bedroom.

When Dad was gone a few times I hid in the basement and watched Becky take showers. She took one every night, and I made sure I was down there before she went to bed.

One of these evenings she must have heard me leaving the basement after she went to bed. The next evening and after that she made sure I was in bed before she went to shower and go to bed. She could have gotten me into a lot of trouble with Dad but she never said a word to him, sparing me a beating.

Becky had assumed the role of being our mother and was hoping that Dad would come back to her. It wasn't going to happen, though. He was mainly living with Helen and her four children.

We were on our own, Becky and we five kids. She took up working at a retail store and training to be a certified nurse.

Becky did the best she could, but there was barely enough food unless Dad surprised us and dropped by. He was spending all his money on Helen and her four kids.

One morning I was down in the basement getting some clean clothes. As I was putting my shirt on I noticed Dad walk past the basement door. It surprised me that he was home and I yelled, "Dad"

He stopped and looked down the stairs at me. I asked him, "Dad, do you have fifty cents so I can eat lunch today?"

There was a bookshelf with a plant on it next to him, and an instant rage came over him. He picked it up and threw it down the stairs.

It was a potted plant in a green vase full of soil. I quickly ducked and it went right past my head, hitting the wall behind me. If I hadn't had such good reflexes, it could have killed me. I stayed in the basement until it was time for school and quietly went up the stairs and headed out of the house.

Dad came up behind me before I could get out and said, "Dave." Then he handed me fifty cents and I quickly left. I can tell you that I never asked him for lunch money again.

I don't know how Becky handled it, but I do thank her. She could have packed up and left with her two daughters. Life was going bad again and it was all because Dad couldn't keep his pants on.

I had very little supervision and started running with the wrong group of people. I was introduced to marijuana and smoked it on a regular basis. Connie and I went into stores and stole cartons of cigarettes to support our habit.

One day my friends and I were in my living room smoking cigarettes when suddenly the front door opened. Dad was standing right in front of me and I had a cigarette in my hand behind my back.

He grabbed my arm, pulled it out in front of me and asked, "When did you start smoking?"

I said, "Two months ago," and he walked away.

The next day when I ran into Becky after school she said, "I didn't know you smoked. Your dad knocked me around because I didn't tell him."

I was allowed to smoke in the house after that but Connie was told to stop. Of course she didn't so she still had to hide it from them.

Danny and I went to an ice skating rink one day and met a couple of girls, Robin and Debbie. I started dating Robin and Danny dated Debbie. When Dad was around he was starting to quiz me about my sex life. He began again with the "It's just a hole with hair around it," and I started believing him again.

I would take Robin out to my clubhouse and almost force her into having sex. She broke up with me one day because I was too persistent in what I wanted from her.

The next day there was a knock at my door. It was Robin's friend Debbie. I let her in and soon we were making out, until Dad showed up.

I asked her to leave, and in about ten minutes knock on my bedroom window. When I heard the knock, I met her at the window and helped her in. Somehow Dad knew what I was up to but he didn't say a word.

When Debbie got into my room wc undressed as quickly as possible and jumped into bed. I didn't waste any time. We had intercourse for about ten minutes.

It wasn't the earth-moving experience Dad had told me it would be. I was actually thinking about Jeannie, while having sex with Debbie. I didn't get the feeling from

Debbie that I was anything special either; she just wanted me to hurry.

When I finished and rolled over, Dad burst in the room and said, "Tell her to leave."

Debbie dressed quickly as Dad watched. I later learned from Debbie that he had watched us doing it the whole time.

Whenever Dad and I went somewhere together alone, he would say, "When you bringing one home for me?"

Debbie and I hooked up to play around and thankfully she didn't get pregnant, because we didn't use protection. I stopped seeing her when she accused Dad of touching her.

I said, "Bullshit. He wouldn't do that."

Becky sat us down one day and said, "Your dad asked me to leave. Kim, Cheri and I are going back to Ohio."

The next thing I knew Becky was gone.

Barbara took on the role of taking care of the house, Connie and me. She cooked with what she had, which wasn't much, mostly sliced up hotdogs and fried potatoes. Barbara stretched what she had and we ate at friends' houses when we could. Barbara didn't have to take on this role, but she did for quite a long time.

Barbara had a boyfriend and said she was going to move in with him. Connie and I packed up all our stuff and Dad put it in storage. Everything we had was put there, never to be seen again. He didn't pay the bill.

Then Dad said, "I'm sending you two to Washington to see your mom for the summer. Barbara will take you to the bus station in a few days. You'll stay with Barbara until then."

A few days later Connie and I got on the Greyhound bus heading for Washington.

CHAPTER 10

TACOMA FOR
THE SUMMER

Connie and I went straight for the rear of the bus and sat down. I wasn't feeling that well, so I slept for a while. Connie woke me up by poking me in the shoulder.

"Do you want to buy some pot?" she whispered in my ear.

I asked, "From who?" and she pointed at a guy that looked like a California surfer.

Dad had given us twenty dollars apiece to buy food for the two-day trip and I knew that was not going to be enough.

I said, "Save your money and buy food with it," so Connie told the surfer, "We don't have that much money."

He opened a large paper grocery store bag and showed it to us. It was half full of marijuana leaves and he started rolling joints right there on the bus. We smoked his pot until we got to Salt Lake City, where he got on another bus heading for California. We headed north to Washington.

The surfer left us about ten joints and they lasted all the rest of the trip. Connie and I smoked in the bus bathroom; that's before they put smoke detectors in them. We went through our twenty bucks quickly and pretty much starved for the last twenty-four hours of the trip.

Mom met us at the bus station when we arrived with bloodshot eyes. She just said, "Hi," didn't hug us, and we put our bags in the trunk of her car.

I remember thinking, *I thought Dad said she wanted us to visit, but I guess he was wrong.*

As Mom drove us to her house she didn't say much except small talk. "How was your trip? Are you hungry? How much money do you have left?"

I noticed that she was driving right smack in the middle of the Black community. I thought, *Damn! Am I going to have to fight all summer?*

Sure enough, she pulled into a driveway in the center of the worst neighborhood in Tacoma.

I carried my bag into the duplex and was given the couch to sleep on for the summer. I ate some dinner and fell asleep.

There was no way I was going to spend my summer fighting every day, so I found Jim's phone number. The next morning I called him, and we picked up right where we had left off as best friends.

I had Mom drive me over to Jim's house the next day, and I started spending the nights there as often as possible. Jim's mom, Suzanne, worked nights as a bartender so we could do what we wanted.

"*Wow!*" is what I thought the first time I saw Laura again. She had grown up. She had a lot of the same features as Jeannie – slim, long brown hair, freckles and a beautiful smile. I thought, *she'll do for the summer.* We hooked up as boyfriend and girlfriend for a short time. But it only lasted a few days. Laura didn't like the idea that I didn't pay much attention to her. I think the pot smoking had something to do with it too, because she didn't smoke.

Soon Jim started introducing me to all his friends. There was one in particular, Greg, who we spent a lot of time with. He could run around at night too, so we did.

I heard Greg say one time, "I can't go. I'm having Terri sneak in my window tonight."

I said, "Terri?"

"Yes," Greg said, "Terri."

I thought, *not my Terri*. Sure enough, Greg was dating the girl I had liked so much in sixth grade. I told him I didn't want to hear anything else about the two of them and he agreed.

That night Jim and I went to the 7-Eleven about eight blocks from his home to play pinball. We were doing really well and kept getting free games. We put in one quarter and played that machine for at least three hours. We finally got so tired of playing it we left over ten credits on it. We started walking home at around two in the morning.

Jim noticed a construction site where a Piggly Wiggly grocery store was being built. We went to investigate what was going on there and to see if we could cause any problems.

Jim said, "I need one of them fluorescent bulbs for my garage."

I lifted him up to get one and we heard a car's brake slam on behind us. I let go of Jim's foot and he fell, shattering the bulb. We turned around to see who was in the car.

It was the police.

We took off running and hid in the bushes behind the store. In just a couple of minutes I had a flashlight shining in my eyes. I stood up and saw Jim with handcuffs on. I turned around and put my arms behind my back as instructed by the officer. We were led to the police car and placed in the back seat. One of the officers radioed to the station, reporting that we were apprehended and back-up officers should be called off. One officer said, "I'll call and see if the construction company wants to press charges."

The answer was yes, so Jim and I were off to Juvenile Hall, and not very happy.

Jim kept saying, "All we did was break a light bulb. This isn't right."

He kept repeating it louder and louder, until one of the officers turned, grabbed him by the hair and said, "Shut up."

I said, "You can't do that!" and he looked at me and replied, "You shut up, too."

We were released the next day to our moms, and did I ever get a tongue lashing.

Jim and I went to court a couple of weeks later and received our sentences. I was made to pay $1.39 restitution and had to wash police cars for forty hours. Jim had the same restitution and had to work in a soup kitchen for the homeless for the same amount of time. Of course we were kept apart until our community service was done.

Another person was doing community service hours washing cars with me at the police station. We would go together to get another police car and, just to rebel, smoke pot in the cars. We would even do drug deals right there at the police station and pad our hours.

If my co-worker didn't show up I would punch his time card and he would do the same for me. I think I actually worked about twenty hours and he put in about the same.

One evening Mom went with her boyfriend to the drive-in movie. Before they left, we washed Mom's car and parked it in the garage.

After she was gone, I called Jim. "Hey, dude, my mom isn't going to be back for a few hours and she left her car keys. You want to go cruising?"

Jim said, "Come get me."

We went cruising that night and did some off-the-road driving as well. The car was a dirty mess when I brought it home and the gas tank was empty. I parked it in the garage just about fifteen minutes before Mom and her boyfriend got home and pretended I was a sleep. I knew I was going to get caught the next morning because it was covered in dirt.

Mom never said a word; she just left in the morning to shop.

A couple of days later I said, "Mom, want me to wash your car? I'm bored and I need something to do."

I wanted to show her what a good son I was.

It was nearing the end of our summer break and I wanted to see Terri before I went back to Omaha. Greg and Terri had broken up and I just wanted to see her. I did have another girlfriend, Lori, who seemed to like me a lot, but she lived so far away we only got together about twice a month. I didn't know it but she was in love with me: later her girlfriend told me. She sent me a letter once I was in Omaha but Dad tore it up.

I met Terri outside her parents' home one day right before we left. We talked for a while, kissed on the lips and I slowly walked away from her.

I was back on the bus with Connie and heading back to Omaha. The bus trip was uneventful and just seemed to drag on. I had an extremely overweight lady sitting next to me most of the trip. She took up her seat and some of mine, leaving me cramped when we finally stopped at the Omaha bus station.

My sister Barbara met us there and she said, "Dad asked us to pick you up. He's busy."

We grabbed our bags and loaded them into the car. Barbara dropped us in front of our new house and quickly drove off.

So Connie and I stood at the door and knocked. Dad answered. He was living with Helen and her four kids. We went inside and I felt right away we weren't wanted there. I was told my bedroom was downstairs in the other boy's room.

The bedroom was set up his way. I couldn't change it around so that my side looked the way I wanted it to. I felt as if I was intruding on his space. We argued just about every time we were in close proximity and I didn't like it there.

Helen, who Dad later married, didn't want us there either and made fun of me every chance she could.

There were times, though, when Helen wanted Connie and me to like her. One of those times was at Barbara and her husband's wedding. We had the reception at our home. Barbara had several people there and his parents flew in from California. There was plenty of beer and some hard alcohol. The adults were downstairs in the den and all of the teenagers, including Connie and I, stayed upstairs on the main floor.

Helen, trying to be nice, kept bringing beer up to us and eventually we all had a buzz going. We were having a great time until Connie ran nose first into a door. Her nose was bleeding really badly and we couldn't get it to stop.

One of us went to get an adult to help her and a few of the adults came upstairs to see what had happened. Dad followed a couple of minutes later and was a bit intoxicated himself. His first thought was that I had punched her and he came at me yelling. He was in my face screaming and I, being drunk, took his challenge. I reared back with my fist and punched him right in his mouth with everything I had. It happened really fast and before I knew it two of the guests took hold of my arms. Dad took the opportunity to punch me back, right in my mouth. The two guests holding my arms then let me loose and held him from hitting me again.

My arms were free now and I threw another punch and landed one, hitting him in the nose. After my second punch they tackled both of us and the fight was over.

When they separated us in different rooms they let me loose. I walked out of the bedroom and for good measure punched a hole in the wall right in front of Connie's face.

The reception ended right then and I went directly to my cousin's for a couple of days to keep us apart. *Wow, I thought, alcohol gave me the courage to stand up for myself.*

From that moment on I drank whenever I could get my hands on alcohol. It brought me out of my shyness and made me feel like I was a normal person. No longer was I going to be pushed around and turn the other cheek. My parents had tormented me enough. I wasn't going to take it any longer. I felt I had crossed the line from being a boy into being a man. I had challenged my dad and hadn't lost.

I didn't like the feeling that Dad and I had finally met toe to toe, but after that he seemed to give me a little respect.

Helen and her kids didn't let up on letting me know I wasn't wanted there, though. I knew Dad had to make the choice of having Helen and her kids over Connie and me. I could see he was torn emotionally because Helen was forcing him to make a decision – us or them.

Through his actions it was clear that Dad wanted them and I decided to move back to Washington state. Dad wasn't the man I knew anymore and it was sad to watch him losing his self-esteem and dignity.

I told Connie, "I'm going back to Washington; you want to go back with me?"

Connie said, "I'm staying here."

That was a very sobering moment as we three kids had always been together. Now my sisters and I wouldn't be able to protect each other anymore.

I called Mom and said, "I want to live in Washington. Can I stay with you?"

It took her a few minutes to answer but she finally said, "I guess."

I went to Dad and told him I missed Washington and I wanted to go back. I saw his eyes immediately tear up and he went to his bedroom. I heard him crying, but it was too late. A couple of days later he handed me a one-way bus ticket to Washington. I packed what little I had and went to the bus station the next day. I had no other communication with Mom, and I was on my way.

The bus stopped in Salt Lake City for a two-hour layover, so I sat on the stairs outside the station. Within a couple of minutes an older man came up, sat next to me and flashed a $20 bill. I knew what he wanted - sexual favors from me. I only like women so I pretended not to notice him.

He said, "Hi," and flashed the twenty dollars again.

I had a buck knife in my sock taped to my leg.

I lifted my pant leg, grabbed the knife and said loudly, "I am not a fag; get the hell away from me!"

I have never seen someone move as quickly as he did making his way out of there. Everyone outside the bus station turned and stared at me holding the knife and him speed-walking away.

I got up and went back into the bus station. There I started talking to a woman who said, "Men come here looking for runaways and most need the money so they target them."

I waited inside the bus station until my bus left for Washington.

I needed a drink and I was able to convince a woman who was over the legal age to buy me some alcohol at one of our stops on the way. The alcohol helped me sleep so I drank and napped all the way to Washington.

When I got to Washington I carried my three suitcases all the way to Mom's duplex, about four miles. I wasn't happy about staying there and I could tell she wasn't too happy about me moving back.

She didn't know what day I was coming and when I reached her door it was open. She was on the phone and I said "Mom" softly through the screen door.

She turned to look and said to the person on the phone, "Dave is here. I have to go."

She rolled her eyes and pointed at a bedroom. "Go put your suitcases in there," she said.

CHAPTER 11

DAMNED IF I DO, DAMNED IF I DON'T

The first thing I did was call Jim. His mom, Suzanne, answered. I learned that Jim was in Alaska working and would be gone for the rest of the summer.

I was really bummed because we lived in a Black neighborhood and I didn't have anything to do. I just sat around watching TV and eating for a week.

Then the phone rang. I wasn't going to answer it but I picked it up on the fourth ring.

It was Jim. "I'm back from Alaska. Let's party!"

Jim had gotten fired early from his job as a cement finisher. He had made enough money to purchase a car and he was on his way to pick me up.

He pulled up in a lime green 1970 Maverick and off we went. He had some beer in a cooler and we drove around looking for a couple of women. That early evening we weren't successful so we headed back to his house.

Suzanne worked the night shift as a bartender, so we threw a party with around twenty people to celebrate Jim's return to Washington.

I started out not being able to talk to the majority of the partygoers because I was so shy. I had a couple of drinks and when the alcohol kicked in I loosened up. If I didn't have a few drinks in me I had a very hard time even saying hello to anyone. I'd be checking out the girls and pick out the one with a pretty face and nice butt.

I was a good looking guy and usually the girls would take a second look. I'd smile, tip my drink and slowly check them out from head to toe. I heard a lot of compliments about my eyes: "Your eyes are beautiful," or "Your eyes pull me right into you." They would usually approach me and if I had a cocktail in me the conversation was on. If I wasn't intoxicated then I might as well forget it. When girls, especially pretty girls, walked up to me they'd say, "Hi." I'd immediately turn red and hardly be able to answer "Hello" back to them. It was as if I was in a glass bubble. The world was revolving around me and I wanted to jump aboard. I felt like I was watching a movie and wasn't a part of the scene. I had absolutely no self-confidence and felt as if I was an outsider.

However, when I drank alcohol I lost that sense of "less than worthy" and could join in the fun around me.

I envied Jim for how he could talk to girls and have so many friends. He took me under his wing and tried to help me become more outgoing. If I had alcohol in me then I was fine with meeting new people. If I was sober then usually I would have rather crawled under a rock and hidden. Often Jim would be standing there talking to someone and I'd struggle to get words out. I didn't have any speech issues, but I was so worried about saying something stupid that there were times when the person would point at me and ask Jim, "Doesn't he talk?"

I'd just look at them and say, "Yes, I talk," and that was about it.

I spent the rest of the summer hanging around Jim day and night. Suzanne didn't mind me staying over, because I could keep Jim in check from being so wild.

Laura and I attempted again a couple of times to be more than just friends but I wanted more than she was willing to give. Laura would walk with me, holding hands, and we'd kiss, but she wasn't letting it go any farther.

I became tired of getting almost there and hearing, "We better stop." I started seeing other girls and Laura and I drifted apart. It wasn't much of a relationship. Most adults would have called it puppy love.

That summer Jim, Greg and I helped move Mom and my half-brothers out of the Black neighborhood. We moved far enough that we weren't the only white people in a one-mile radius. I could go outside now without having to fight all the time.

Jim, Greg and I partied the rest of the summer until school started.

Jim lived too far away so when school started we could only get together about every other weekend. I started the eleventh grade and took a city bus to go to a primarily White school.

Foss High was middle class so most of the eleventh and twelfth graders had their own cars or they drove their parents' cars. I went on a mission to get my driver's license so I would have a chance with the girls. I failed the written part the first time but studied harder and passed the second try. I passed the driving test the first time and earned my driver's license.

Mom rarely let me drive her car unless I begged for hours or she needed something from the store. I needed my own car so one day I went walking the business district putting in applications at restaurants.

The phone rang a couple of days later and I was offered a dishwashing job only three blocks away from where we lived. I took the job and worked the weekends, earning enough money to save up to buy myself some new clothes and go out on dates.

I liked working at the dinner-theatre where, with a chef's hat on my head, I would cut the meat on the smorgasbord line, then serve coffee and bus the tables during the theatre plays. Once the play was over I'd go into the kitchen and finish up dishwashing with the dishwasher.

I was called into the office one Saturday evening and told to sit down.

The owner told me that a theatre critic had attended the previous weekend's dinner and I was in the newspaper's write-up.

He read, "The meals were great and David never let the coffee get cold."

Then he gave me a quarter raise and said, "Keep up the good work."

I left his office proud and at the same time relieved. I had thought he was going to fire me because I was stealing booze out of the liquor cabinet. I would close up after everything was cleaned for the next day and then grab a fifth of whiskey on the way out the door. I needed it to function at school and put up with Mom. I seldom smoked marijuana anymore so booze was my only escape from reality.

I hated going home from school or work because Mom treated me very demandingly. Here I was sixteen years old and it was as if I had a dog collar on me. I felt as though I was being used like a slave. I had a curfew at dusk, and if I had downtime Mom would have me do some kind of work to control me and amuse herself: wash the windows, do the dishes, vacuum the floor…

I was a typical teenager who thought I knew everything. We had terrible arguments and I had to leave at times to cool down.

I came home from school on one Fall day and found out that Connie was having it rough in Omaha and had decided to move back to Washington. I felt good that we were together again, but also felt bad for her because she didn't know what she was getting into.

We were invited over to Grandma's for a Christmas dinner in 1979. Uncle John, Mom, Connie, Steve, Loyd and I along with Jim's family were there. Barbara was in Omaha and it was the first time we three didn't spend Christmas together.

Grandma as usual cooked up a nice feast for everyone. It was my first year to sit at the adult table; it would have been sooner but I had been gone for many years. Our family tradition was to have the adults sit at one table and the kids at the other.

When everyone finished we all sat around in the living room and exchanged gifts. As everyone was opening gifts I heard my cousin say, to my mom, "Thanks Aunt Marsha for the diary."

A minute or so later I heard her say, "Aunt Marsha, someone already wrote in this."

I knew that Mom had bought all her gifts at the Goodwill and I said, "Mom, you could have at least checked to see if someone had wrote in it already."

Mom didn't say a word, she just continued on like she didn't hear us.

I had my car and Connie, Erika, Erick and I took off and went to the bowling alley. We played pool, video games and went back to Grandma's a couple hours later. I believe that was the last Christmas both families have spent together with the majority of us there.

The pressure was mostly off of me now because Mom started picking on Connie. Connie soon found that out and tried to stay away as much as I did. She was able to get a job at the age of fifteen on a school pass. She started working at a fast food restaurant after school.

I was doing homework one evening and Connie walked in the door from work. She had a smile on her face, and said, "Guess who walked in my work and ordered some food?"

I asked "Who?" and she said, "Cara. Mom used to baby-sit her on East I street."

I thought for a moment, not remembering her, then asked, "What does she look like?"

Connie said, "Cute. She's blonde and short and thin."

I told Connie to get her phone number and tell her I'd take her out if she wanted.

A couple of days later Connie handed me Cara's phone number and said, "She wants to go out with you. Call her."

I phoned her and we set a date for the following Thursday. I begged Mom to let me use her car and she agreed only because she wanted to see Cara.

Cara had her sister Debra drop her off at our house around six. I had Connie answer the door and Cara walked in. Wow! She was prettier than I imagined her to be. She stood no more than five feet tall and had blue eyes.

We sat for a short time while Cara reminisced with Mom. The whole time I grew more anxious to get going.

We finally took off. I had my booze in a Coke bottle with a little Coke in it so nobody knew. We drove around most of the time, stopping at a park and talking. It was getting near my curfew time and while driving around I put the move on her.

I leaned over, kissed her and asked, "What now?"

She said, "I know this place we can park."

I followed her directions to a dark dead-end street and we made out for a while in the front seat. I started undressing her, expecting her to stop me at any time. We crawled over the front seats and did what comes naturally until it was time to drop her off.

The next day she broke up with her long-distance boyfriend and we became boyfriend and girlfriend.

I spent all the free minutes I had with Cara after that. I'd go to school, take the bus to her sister's place, walk home ten miles in the dark and only sleep at home. We became a perfect match as she was shy, too.

On the weekends I saw Cara before work and I would find a way to hook up with her after I clocked out. She lived with her sister Debra because of abuse from her father, Perk. Debra had a boyfriend and was hardly ever home.

Life was very good at this time. I hardly had to see Mom and had enough cash to keep our budding relationship going.

Mom realized that I was happy now and tried to put a stop to it. Soon she wouldn't let me use her car, tried to keep me home all the time and tried to take all the money I made from working.

One day in the spring of 1979 I came home from school and packed up most of the clothes I owned. I called Jim and had him ask Suzanne if I could live there.

He called me back and said, "She said 'Yes' as long as you stay in school."

I moved in with Suzanne, Jim and Laura and told Mom, "See you. I'm not coming back."

I kept my job for the rest of the schoolyear and graduated from the eleventh grade. Then I quit my job. I started seeing Cara less and less. Jim and I had found a liquor store that wasn't alarmed and we could jimmy the back window open. We broke into it several times getting cases of booze. We threw parties at Jim's house usually having lots of people there.

I soon broke it off with Cara and started falling back into my own world.

When the liquor store realized they were getting alcohol stolen; they put up bars around their windows and we had to find another source. We found a lounge within a couple of days and kept the parties going. We were smarter this time and only took four or five half gallons at a time. It was a little riskier though. We had to wait until they closed late at night and jimmy their door open with a bank card. It was on a busy street so we parked in front of the door, opened the door really fast, grabbed the booze and drove away as fast as possible.

Jim only did this half the time because I insisted. I needed the booze to socialize and even just to talk to the girls.

Cara wasn't about to give up on us though, and I had her come over now and then just for sex. I treated her really badly and I have no idea why she kept trying.

Cara and Jim talked for hours each night and she thought Jim's motive was to get her and me back together. It wasn't; he wanted in her pants. I finally told him hands off and he became sincere in helping Cara and me renew our relationship.

One night when Jim and I were talking he finally convinced me to call her and we got back together. I did tell her that Jim and I were still going to hang out together and she wasn't always going to be with us.

One night Jim and I borrowed Jim's uncle's car and cruised around all night. We needed some gas money and went into the back window of a barber shop to get a few bucks.

Someone walking by spotted us and called the police. We were caught trying to drive away and Jim and I were busted. They took us to a juvenile facility and we spent the weekend locked up. I was ordered to go back to Mom's and put on one-year probation.

I reported weekly to my probation officer and generally we talked about my home life.

I did what I was supposed to do and even tried to make it livable at home. Mom ordered me to do everything around the house. If I protested she said, "Do it or I'll send you back to jail."

Cara and I were sitting in my bedroom talking one afternoon when Mom came to my door.

Smirking, she said, "Cara, you have to go home now. David has work to do."

I stood up and protested, "She just got here."

Mom said, "Leave now or David's going to jail."

I couldn't take it anymore and said, "Fuck you. I'm leaving."

She grabbed the phone and called the police. "My son's on probation," she told them, "and I want you to come pick him up."

I gathered as many clothes as I could carry, destroyed everything else in my room, and quickly left.

I stayed at Cara's that night and called my probation officer the next morning. He told me to come in that afternoon and I'd have to go in front of the judge.

My probation officer and I talked a little before going in front of the judge. I thought I was going to have to spend some time behind bars.

Then he said, "I'm going to request emancipation. Is that what you want?"

I said, "Yes, I'll make it somehow."

I watched as Mom entered the courtroom and sat behind me. I looked at her and she smirked at me as we made eye contact.

She thought I was going to spend a few days in jail and have to go back home with her.

The judge asked me to stand and he said, "I have spoken with your probation officer. I wouldn't do this if you were a female." He picked up his gavel and went on to say, "You're on your own, boy. Stay out of trouble. I'm emancipating you."

I looked back at Mom. She had a shocked look on her face. I winked at her and she stood up and stormed out of the courtroom.

The judge looked at me and said, "Good luck. I don't want to ever see you back here again."

I said, "You won't." Then I thanked my probation officer and left and caught a bus to Jim's house.

Suzanne agreed to let me stay there as long as I got a job or went to school.

Cara and I started seeing each other more and more and she convinced her dad, Perk, to get me a job at AMVETS where he was post commander. I cleaned up after the bingo games, dances and parents-without-partners events. I'd come in around 6 AM on the weekends and have the place to myself.

It wasn't a bad job but I had to start out hitchhiking around four in the morning to get there in time. I'd get the place cleaned up within four or five hours and then jimmy open the side door of the bar and start drinking. I ate pepperoni sticks, played the pull tabs and got drunk.

Then I washed my glass and made it look undisturbed from the previous night.

I was able to save enough money to buy my first car, a 1969 Buick Skylark. I felt very good about how my life was going. I had a job, a car and a nice place to live. I also had a girl who loved me, and I planned on staying in school to receive my high school diploma.

I was at Cara's one afternoon when Jim called. "Dave, I just got kicked out of the house and we can't go back."

Jim went to stay at a friend's house and I immediately became homeless. I crawled into Cara's basement window to sleep for a couple of nights, trying to decide what I was going to do. The next Saturday morning I went to work and, after cleaning up, I went into the bar. I had quite a few drinks in me when I noticed the cash box.

I opened it and counted the money. There was over $500 and some change. I put the money in my pocket and walked out the door. The next day I called my boss and quit.

He asked me to bring the money back and I said, "I don't know what you're talking about." Then I hung up the phone.

I didn't hear any more about it for quite some time. All my plans were shattered now and I didn't have any idea what I was going to do.

CHAPTER 12

HOMELESS

I look back on this time of my life and wonder how I ever survived. Fortunately it was summer and I had Cara and my car. I found places to park at night and would crawl in the back with my blanket and go to sleep. A few times I woke up with someone tapping my window. I'd sit up and see a police officer standing there and have to get out of my car.

I could see in their eyes that they didn't like what they saw, a teenager sleeping in his car, but they had their job to do.

They would always say, "You can't sleep here. You'll have to move somewhere else."

I'd oblige them and go to some other area that was dark and try to get back to sleep. I didn't feel safe or comfortable sleeping in my car but I had no other choice. The only times I slept in a bed was when Cara let me crawl through her bedroom window. Perk, Cara's dad, seemed to always know when I was there and most of the time didn't bother me. I found out later that he figured out where I parked my car on the other block and when he went to work he would see it. He also told me later that when his alarm clock went off at six in the morning, he would go to his bedroom window and see me walking down the alley.

For a while I also pitched a tent in their backyard and sometimes crawled in there for the night. Then one day it was stolen so back to my car I went.

The only reason I survived was because of Cara and Perk. Cara worked the evening shift at a fast food restaurant. I went there after the owner left at around four and Cara cooked what I wanted. I'd sit there in the dining area because I had nowhere else to go and stay until she clocked out.

When Cara and the other worker went in the back to count the register money, I'd reach behind the register and grab the cigarette machine keys. I'd open it up and grab a few packs and quickly put the keys back.

One time one of the other workers came out and saw me with the machine open. I froze. She smiled and said, "That's okay; take what you want."

She had a crush on me and often asked me when we were going to get together. I kept turning her down but that just made her try harder.

She and many of Cara's girlfriends flirted with me and I could have slept with most of them. I did flirt back but I felt loyalty towards Cara and didn't want to hurt her.

I found some odd jobs to do but it was never enough to keep gas in my car. Cara gave me gas money on her paydays but I needed more.

One day I asked Cara to get me the keys from her dad to AMVETS. She refused for a few days, but I kept insisting. One night she wrote me a note saying something similar to, "I'll do this for you but I want some new clothes when you get the money."

I agreed and the next night she handed me the keys from her bedroom window. Perk was the post commander; he always left his key ring on the coffee table.

I set it up for Jim to meet me near AMVETS and we parked our cars about a block away. We entered AMVETS after they closed and went directly to the bar area. We noticed that they put a chain from one side of the door to the other and wondered how we could get at the cash box.

I found a hammer and started knocking holes in the hollow door until it was big enough to crawl through. We went into the little storage room and there sat a laundry basket full of cement with the safe sitting right in the middle.

We couldn't carry it so we had to go get a sledgehammer. About an hour later we came back and busted up the cement until the safe was loose, then we left with it.

We drilled the bottom of the safe until we could get the money out. There was about $400 and we split it. Then we took the safe to a bridge and threw it into the river. I went back to Cara's bedroom window, gave her the keys and went off with Jim.

I was at Cara's the next day when Perk walked in with tears in his eyes. He looked directly at me and said, "Someone broke into AMVETS again last night."

I knew he knew it was me but I wasn't going to admit it. He just went up to his room and Cara and I left.

Connie got hold of me somehow that day and said, "Dad's here in Tacoma and has an apartment on 38th Street."

Cara and I went over there and knocked on his door.

He said, "I've been looking for you. You're moving in here if you want."

It was only a couple of blocks from Cara's house and of course I said, "Sure."

I had my own bedroom and Dad had the other. Connie soon moved in and Dad made the couch his bed. Dad was really trying because he knew he had made the wrong choice in picking Helen and her kids over us.

It was only a few days after I broke into AMVETS that Cara called me. "My dad found the note I wrote to you and I'm at the police station. They want to have you call them."

I said, "I'll call them later today. Meet me at your mom's in a couple of hours."

We met there and Cara told her mom and Perk everything. Perk turned me in and made sure Cara was left out of it.

I told Dad and he wasn't happy. But he only said, "I wish I had moved up here a couple of weeks earlier."

I called up the detective and told him I'd be in on Monday. He agreed.

There was one problem though – I was seventeen when we broke in there and now I was eighteen. Now I was an adult looking at prison time.

On Monday the detective gave me two choices. "Confess and we'll try to talk the judge into making this a juvenile offense," he said, "or we'll place you in as an adult and book you into Pierce County jail."

I took the confession route and, when all was said and done, received thirty days in the juvenile facility.

Perk kept telling Cara I was getting a few years and she should forget about me. He had a surprised look on his face when I drove up to his house four weeks later.

That scared me enough that I started looking for work and stayed away from my rebellious friends. I went back to school and lived with Dad and Connie.

We all chipped in on food when we had money but there really wasn't enough. I went half of my senior year, but was going to be a few credits short of graduating. I always had a bottle of whiskey in my car and went to take shots between classes.

Since I was eighteen, I started not going to class and then I dropped out. However I did get my GED, one month later, passing it on my first try.

Our apartment had two recliners, a TV, two beds and a few kitchen items. The TV was rented from Rent-A-Center, and I often saw them drive up, trying to take it back because Dad couldn't pay. They did take it one day, but we somehow found a nineteen-inch color TV so we used that.

Cara asked to talk to me one day alone and we went for a drive. She said, "I don't like to wait for you at your place when you're not there."

I asked, "Why?"

She said, "Your dad always traps me in a corner and tries to press up against me."

I said, "I don't believe you. Don't tell me that!"

I wasn't street smart enough to know it, but my dad had set his "Master Plan" into action. Cara had a lot of good looking girlfriends and they came over with Cara quite often. When they left, Dad always said, "You're too young to be tied down. Them girls like you, too."

I wasn't thinking in that way but he kept instilling it into my mind.

Dad had been married and divorced six or seven times by the time he hit his mid-forties. I'm sure now that he wasn't giving me the best advice because I always wanted one wife, kids and a white picket fence in front of our home. He was going to make sure that didn't happen for me, though.

It wasn't long until Jim, with Dad's encouragement, was bringing girls over to meet me.

One day Cara got fed up with Dad's advances and said, "If you're not going to do anything about it, I think we should see other people."

I asked for advice from Dad and he told me I should split up with Cara. She wanted me to say "no" to seeing other people but, taking Dad's advice, we broke up.

Jim came over one evening with a couple of girls and I started dating one of them, Debbie Brigham – a blonde who stood about five feet seven. We hit it off really quickly. Debbie was very attractive and it wasn't long before we were an item. I had a problem though. Cara wanted to get back together. But I was having too much fun and there were girls for me every night of the week.

I had a hard time being faithful to Debbie so I told her we should just be friends.

Jim wanted his shot at Debbie and we set a plan in action. I was going to avoid Debbie and Jim would pick up the slack by talking to her. He would tell her he would pick her up and they would come looking for me. I was to get jealous of them being together and not want anything to do with her.

The plan went down perfectly except that Debbie didn't fall for Jim afterwards and he didn't get into her pants.

Debbie was told a different story by Jim, but she and I remain friends to this day.

It was a free-for-all with me now, seeing as many girls as I could handle. I also felt good that I didn't have to cheat to have them over.

It wasn't long before most of the girls I was seeing started telling Cara and it was hurting her badly. I had been to bed with a few of her friends and several girls that I had met through Jim before my conscience started bothering me.

Dad always made sure that I had a bottle of whiskey and beer for the girls when they came over. He kept giving me stiff drinks and the girls more and more beer. He hoped to have me pass out and have the girls buzzed enough to have sex with him. It never worked, though, because with my high tolerance I never passed out, and I always made sure the girls were with me when I went to bed.

Cara wanted us back together again. Dad had her come over while I wasn't there and always put the moves on her. He let her cry on his shoulder and then tried to take advantage of her weakness. She never fell for his advances, though.

But I found out later that one of my girlfriends did. I kept hearing, "Your dad's is a dirty old man."

I got used to it, saying, "Yeah, I know. What can I do about it?"

It soon became clear to me that Dad was trying to live his youth again through me and was jealous of me. Once the lightbulb went off in my head I could see how much he wanted his youth back and envied everything I did.

One day I was at school waiting to pick up Cara. As she walked towards my car out of the blue one of the girls I was sleeping with, Kim, walked up to her, only a few feet away. They started talking and soon there were tears flowing down Cara's face. I didn't know what to do so I just let them talk. Cara looked at me, crying, then turned and walked away. Getting out of my car I followed her.

We didn't talk for a day or two but we both decided that we shouldn't date other people anymore.

Dad did convince me, though, that girls on the side didn't hurt anything, so I kept sleeping with them. A few times Cara came over earlier than planned and I'd have girls leaving. I was getting pulled two separate ways: Cara wanting to be monogamous and Dad wanting me to sleep with as many girls as I could.

I always felt proud the next morning after the girls left, and it made me feel more like a man.

Dad told me, "You're giving them what they want," and "Tell them what they want to hear."

I knew I was hurting these girls by making promises that I had no intention of keeping. I kept hearing from Dad, "They're just a hole with hair around it. Just don't get them pregnant."

I had a really hard time juggling the girls around so they didn't come over all at once and let my secret out of the bag. Dad always helped me out there. If one girl and I were together, he'd say I wasn't there. Then he would ask them if they wanted to go get dinner or go for a ride.

I started feeling badly about what I was doing. Some of the girls let me have their virginity. It was really hard looking into their eyes after using them and knowing it was just a fleeting moment for me.

I sometimes got drunk and then Dad asked me for details about these women. Sometimes, drunkenly, I would tell him. I knew deep in my heart that they weren't just "holes with hair around it" but they seemed to be throwing themselves at me and it was hard to stop myself.

Cara and I knew it was time for us to get our own place and get away from Dad's influence and near-rapes. I finally went to work at an ice factory, stacking pallets of bagged ice. I worked as much as possible and soon we had enough money saved up. We ended up moving into a duplex that was half-furnished. Although struggling because we both made minimum wage, at least I wasn't homeless. I wasn't going to cheat on Cara after moving in together and was prepared mentally to remain faithful and start a family in a couple of years.

I was sitting on our couch while Cara was at work just a couple of days after we moved in when I heard a car pull up. Soon there was a knock at the door.

I answered the door and there stood one of the women I had slept with - I had taken her virginity.

Kim had a bottle of Black Velvet and a big smile, and she said, "Your dad told me where you moved to. Do you mind if I come in?"

I stood there for a couple of minutes, looking at her in her tight jeans, her blouse unbuttoned halfway, knowing it was the wrong thing to do. Then I said, "Come on in. Pour me a drink."

She walked in and I closed the door behind her.

I said quietly under my breath, "Dad, you're an asshole!"

CHAPTER 13

A HOME OF OUR OWN AND ASHLEY ARRIVES

I sat there drinking and kept telling myself, "I'm not going to sleep with her. I've changed and want more out of life."

Then I heard Dad's voice in my head: "You're not married. Go for it."

Kim and I chatted for a while. Finally she asked me, "You going to show me around your place?" She stood up and grabbed my hand. "Where's the bedroom?"

I stood, too, thinking, "*Oh, heck, one more for the road.*"

I took her straight to the bedroom, and we did our thing, I then had to practically push her out the door before Cara got home.

Our place soon became the party house for all of our friends on the weekends. I went to work every day and saved my drinking for the weekends. Cara's mom once told me I was a weekend alcoholic. I felt good when she said that because in most people's minds I only drank during the weekend. Little did they know I was still drinking almost every night. However, I wasn't getting so drunk I'd pass out. I only had a couple of drinks a night.

I pretty much went to work every day for the next year and stayed out of trouble. We entertained friends at our house so it kept me in check.

We stayed at the duplex for six months and then moved into a quadruplex to save money.

I felt pretty good about just flirting and was able to be satisfied by Cara.

One night Cara and I were throwing a party and one of the couples left. Five minutes later they came running in the door yelling.

"Some guy tried to rape me!" the girl shouted.

I asked, "Where?"

They took me outside and pointed at the car a half block down the road. I took off running toward the car, then a bigger guy jumped me and we started fighting. He put me down fast and started punching me while I tried to fight back.

Cara ran up and tried to pull him off of me and a large woman started punching her.

Cara and I ran back to the apartment and I grabbed a baseball bat. I yelled to everyone, "Let's go kick some ass!"

I took off out the door and several guys followed me.

The guy and woman leaped into their car but it flooded and wouldn't start. I calmly walked up to the car, looked right into the driver's eyes, and put the bat through the windshield. I continued to beat the car until all the lights and windows were broken. Then for good measure I beat the hood a couple of times.

They finally got their car started, sped off and called the police. When the police came they took statements but nothing ever happened.

I saw the car at a body shop the next day; it was totaled.

One night as I was doing my taxes I figured out how much Cara and I would get back if we were married.

Hmm, a thousand more. I stood up from the table and walked over to Cara.

I went down on one knee and asked, "Will you marry me?"

She had always wanted to, so I knew the answer was going to be yes.

She said, "Yes."

We set the date for a few months down the road and went on with our lives.

The marriage was called off once when Cara admitted to meeting a guy after a party at a park and made – out with him in her car. I asked her to move out of the apartment and she left about one week later. I had turned 21 and had been promoted to foreman at my job, making more money. I now had the bachelor pad and my place became the hangout for my friends. It wasn't long though before Cara and I reconciled and we moved into a nice two bedroom house with a large yard and garage.

Cara had gotten out of the fast food field and found a job working at a trucking company. We both were making more money and I had enough money to pay more rent and build muscle cars. Life was pretty good and we both were on our way to the good life. I still wanted to get out with the guys once in awhile but Cara insisted that I couldn't go without her.

One Friday a few of my friends wanted to go out and I knew I would have a hard time convincing Cara to let me go.

I remembered that my Dad would come home and throw his plate of food at the wall and storm out and it always worked for him.

I came home that early evening and Cara placed my plate of spaghetti in front of me.

I yelled, "Spaghetti again!" and threw it against the kitchen wall.

I stood up quickly and started to go out the door. She stood in front of the door and shouted, "You're not going anywhere until you clean up that mess!"

It had backfired on me and I ended up cleaning up my mess and not going out. It was the first and last time I ever threw my food, not because I had to clean it up but

I remember seeing Becky cry when Dad threw his plate. I saw the pain in Becky's eyes and didn't want Cara to feel that pain.

We were married in a church a few months later and threw a large reception. Jim was my best man and Cara's sister, Debra, was her bridesmaid. It happened that Terri, who I was still very fond of, was Jim's date for our wedding. It was a great wedding and reception and everyone had a tremendous time. It was a bit difficult for me, though, because I had both my new wife and Terri there. I managed to not make a fool of myself flirting with Teri and the reception ended without incident.

We went on our honeymoon into Canada for a few days and talked about starting a family. When we returned home we went shopping for a house and purchased one a few months later. We were both excited to move into our first home that we bought for ourselves. It was a two-story and I turned the upstairs into a game room. We had a pool table, electronic dartboard and a two-player sit down Asteroids machine. I also had antique beer signs with a beer keg cooler. We quickly turned it into the house for our friends to party at on the weekends.

One morning as I was getting in my car to go to work, Barry, who stood around six five and had red hair to the middle of his back, introduced himself. He and his family lived next door to the south of us. I had seen his wife and two young sons but we hadn't talked.

Barry and I had a lot of the same interests and soon we became friends.

I still worked at the ice factory and was getting tired of it. Barry suggested that I get into the heating, venting and air-conditioning field (HVAC) as it paid more.

Barry was lead installer at a large grocery store being built and needed a helper. I soon quit my job at the ice factory and went on unemployment for a short time.

I grew tired of being broke and bored so Barry hired me as an installer. I had very little experience as a sheet metal technician so Barry took me under his wing and taught me the trade.

One evening Barry brought his wife, Kathryn, over and introduced her to us. They were going dancing and asked if we wanted to go out with them.

Kathryn was very pleasant to look at and had a nice smile. We went out with them that evening and had a great time. The two women got along great together and soon we four were all going out clubbing or they would come over and shoot pool or darts.

One day Barry told me that he took a job out of state that would last about a year but they would be returning. He had taught me enough about the HVAC field so I continued it as my career.

Now I had a better-paying job working in the HVAC field and I loved it. I worked at least twelve hours a day, including Saturdays.

I quickly became a lead installer and put everything into my work. I was the best in the company at installing furnaces and water heaters. I was very proud to look at my work after completing it and think, "*Damn, I'm good!*"

I took guys who were just hired, not knowing what a pipe wrench was, and within a few months had trained them to install water heaters and furnaces on their own.

I wouldn't get home until late at night and my helpers hated me for keeping them out so late, but I didn't care. I looked forward to going into the office the next morning and getting that "Atta boy" from the owner. The business went from two trucks when I started there to over twenty-three when I quit five years later.

In the last couple years the company had turned into a drug haven and the quality of work from most of the other installers was very poor. I'm very surprised that no homeowners ever got blown up in their homes from a gas explosion, but I do know of one restaurant that caught fire. The HVAC owners didn't seem to care. They were raking in the cash. I was paid well but the majority of the other installers were making just above minimum wage.

Cara and I were doing pretty well financially and everything was going very well. It was probably because I was seldom home. I would just drop off my paycheck in the morning on payday and hustle off to work.

Cara needed more and I did, too. We decided to start a family and she quit her job.

We tried very hard to have a baby but Cara was having a difficult time getting pregnant.

Then one morning I was sleeping and she woke me up. She said, "The test says I'm pregnant."

We started making up the baby's room to get it prepared and I watched as her belly grew almost daily.

One day after I came home from work she was crying. I asked, "What's wrong?"

Cara said, "My dad has liver cancer and there's nothing they can do."

(We were hoping that he would live to see our baby, but he passed away the day before her due date.)

Ashley was born two weeks later, in February, 1987.

Ashley was a beautiful baby, blonde and blue eyed, and I wanted her to have everything. I continued to work long hours and brought home as much money as I could.

She did have everything material. The problem was I missed those first couple of years of her life because I was working.

I could only kiss her while she slept as I was leaving for work, then look forward to kissing her again when I got home at night.

One night I fell asleep on the couch. At about two in the morning I woke up, opened my eyes and saw a head about two feet from me. It was a man with a medium beard and a scowl on his face. I stared at him for a few seconds and all he did was stare back at me with a mean look. I was really scared and clenched my eyes shut for a couple of seconds.

When I opened my eyes again the head was gone. I crawled into bed with Cara and called in sick that morning.

I went to the library that day and checked out a book on ghost hauntings. I was reading the book when the phone rang. It was Mom and she said, "Guess what happened?'

I immediately said, "Buck died!"

She asked how I knew and I told her, "He came to me last night."

I hated that man enough that I had always promised myself that when I was big enough I would go to Missouri and kick his butt. I soon realized that he had come to me to ask for forgiveness. I figured he had that mean look on his face because my hatred prevented him from going towards the Light. Perhaps he went towards the Light but God told him he had unfinished business on Earth. I know it was real, but you can draw your own conclusions on why or if he was really there.

It took me about six months before I gave Buck my forgiveness and let his soul go from my hatred. Where he is now is anyone's guess; he made his own bed to lie in.

I put my whole life into my family and work.

Then it happened. Dad found out where I lived and he was homeless. We let him stay upstairs and while I was at work he kept trying to get into Cara's pants. I talked to him a few times about it but he didn't care. He even went so far as to say that Ashley wasn't mine.

I had to ask him to leave a few times but he always came back in a few months with no place to live.

He tried to put the idea into my head that Cara was sleeping around on me, and I fought it for a while. But

I eventually started believing that maybe she was. I began to notice that she was wearing shorter shorts than she normally wore and going braless. So I figured if she was sleeping around, so could I.

One day while Cara was with her mom and I had the day off, a woman knocked on the door selling magazines. I invited her in and she showed me the selection.

I was in a good mood so I purchased *Sports Illustrated* for a two-year subscription.

The woman said, "The more points I earn the closer I get to winning a free trip to the Bahamas."

I said, "Oh, then you can run down the beach naked."

She got a look in her eyes - I knew that look.

I leaned over and kissed her.

We had sex right there on the couch. When we finished she simply got dressed and said, "Thanks for the good time and enjoy your magazine."

She did call me a couple times to see me again but I felt guilty and tried to forget her. It was hard though because every week I received a new magazine in the mail and it reminded me of her.

Cara finally had found a job to help with the bills along with her expensive shopping habit. Cara wouldn't come home from work right away and I had to cut my hours back to watch Ashley. We had a sitter but it was expensive so sometimes one of us took the day off to babysit.

One day I came home from work and Cara had her girlfriend over. Cara had taken the day off to watch Ashley. The table was stacked with empty beer cans and I grabbed one from the refrigerator. I said hello to Corrie and winked at her. She looked really hot and I thought, *wow!*

Corrie left soon after I arrived. Cara came up to me about an hour later and suggested we have a threesome.

It took me a few seconds to answer, wondering if it was a trick question, and then I said, "Sure." We had talked about having a threesome before but I didn't think she was serious.

We planned for the event to happen two weeks later after they had a girls' night out.

I counted down the days until the evening arrived. When the day finally arrived, they took off for the evening and I wondered if it would really happen.

I got a sitter for Ashley and came home. Waiting in anticipation, I went to bed and turned on the TV.

Cara and Corrie came home late that night. While I lay there in bed, Cara put in an XXX-rated movie. Corrie walked in and they both undressed as I watched, not saying a word. Then they crawled into bed with me.

Every so often Cara surprised me with another woman and I never turned her down. We were having fun but it did take its toll on our marriage. Soon there was no trust there and the marriage started falling apart.

Cara told me one Friday that she and her friends wanted to go out for a girls' night on the town. I didn't have a problem with that and called one of my friends. The girls took off one way that night and we took off the other.

After a night of shooting pool and having a few beers we went to meet the girls at a local tavern. We were supposed to meet them there around one AM but showed up an hour early.

When we walked in I noticed all four of the girls slow dancing with four guys on the dance floor. The rest of the tavern was empty other than the bartender.

As soon as Cara saw me she immediately stopped dancing and went to her table. I sat down next to her and put my cigarette out in her beer. Then the bartender came up to me and shouted, "Get out of here"

I picked up the beer glass that was nearly full and tossed it in his face. At that time I noticed my friend going outside with the four guys to fight.

I followed them to have the odds more even but he didn't need me. One guy was already out cold on the ground and when I came out to fight two guys ran and the other dragged off his friend.

We jumped in my Blazer and sped off before the police could get there.

Cara didn't come home that night and moved in with Corrie, taking Ashley with her. She later rented her own apartment and we stayed separated for six month before she moved back.

I bought a motorcycle and began not to care anymore. I enjoyed riding for hours with the warm air in my face and rode whenever I had the time.

Cara and I argued all the time and it took its toll on Ashley.

One day Ashley told me, "I wish you would move."

She was only five but I knew she was right. It broke my heart and I wondered why I had worked so hard for it just to be over like this.

Cara and I discussed it and we both decided she couldn't afford to keep the house, so she and Ashley would get an apartment.

I started to drink more and more and we both knew it was over. I wanted to be free, and I insisted that Cara get out as soon as possible. It wasn't long before she granted me my wish.

CHAPTER 14

MIGHT AS WELL LIVE IT UP

I woke up that morning as if it was just going to be a normal day. I took my shower, got dressed and kissed Ashley as she lay there sleeping. I drove off to work, listening to the radio and munching on some Fritos. As usual I cleaned out my truck from the job I had done the day before and went into the office to get the day's work. After I filled my coffee cup, I looked over the paperwork and told my helper what to load. I'd make sure we had enough fittings, sheet metal, and gas pipe to complete the job.

On this day I had two light jobs in the Tacoma area so I gave my helper to another crew. I could do them myself and I preferred working alone if there wasn't much heavy lifting.

I finished the first job around eleven and headed for my next job. Home was on the way, so I decided to make a pit stop for lunch.

When I arrived, I saw a U-Haul truck backed up to the front door. I waited a few minutes in my truck and collected myself. I didn't want to go in there angry but I knew Cara was leaving with Ashley. I made my way around the U-Haul and walked into the front door. Cara's whole family were there throwing everything into the truck as fast as they could.

Everyone stopped when they saw me. Their mouths dropped and their eyes opened wide when I started walking towards them.

Cara was holding a box in her arms in the living room and I slowly went up to her. When I was within a foot of her I had a sad smile on my face.

I said, "Please leave the house keys on the kitchen counter when you're done and lock it up."

She nodded a "yes" and I turned and left.

The rest of the day was long for me and I finished the job around five o'clock, the whole time thinking, "What will I have left?"

I had worked my butt off working at least sixty hours a week to buy nice things and I was sure it was all going to be gone.

Sure enough when I walked in the front door that evening all I could see was my television sitting on the floor and a couch in the living room. In my bedroom Cara had left my clothes and most of my personal items on the floor. The kitchen had some old pots and pans and enough place settings for two. She was nice about it though; she had left me a phone and my electronic dart board.

I ordered pizza that night and fell asleep on the couch.

I had worked so hard for a traditional life: two cars, a home, raising a family and money in the bank. I waited for a couple of days and then called Cara to ask about Ashley and to let her know it was final. There would be no moving back and our marriage was finished.

I then took a day off work and bought an entertainment center to put my TV on. I decided the couch would do for now to sleep on. Dad came over every night and urged me not to talk to "that bitch." I needed some time anyway so she and I didn't talk for a few weeks.

One evening Dad said, "I saw your old girlfriend Kim last night and she wants your phone number."

This piqued my interest and I said, "Give it to her."

Kim called me about an hour later and I invited her over. When she got there she looked over my whole house, and then said, "You don't have a bed. I am not staying here tonight. You're going furniture shopping with me tomorrow. How much money do you have?"

I responded, "Plenty," and she left, saying, "I'll be back tomorrow around ten or so to help you pick it out."

The next day we went to Levitz Furniture and I picked out a black lacquer bedroom set and a kitchen table. I took the bedroom set home that day to sleep on that night.

When I had set it up even I was impressed about how good it looked. Kim came over later that night and cuddled up with me keeping me warm. I gave her a house key before I went to work on Monday. She wanted us to get back together from fifteen years ago when I had "turned her into a woman."

Kim and I lasted a few days until the word got out: "Cara left Dave. He's single." I had quite a few women calling me quizzing me about my newfound freedom. I wasn't ready to jump into a relationship again so soon and wanted to explore my options.

One day after work I walked into my house and saw Kim had put up pictures of her son. I knew that she was trying to move in and I put a stop to it right away.

I handed her some money and said, "This isn't working," and asked for my key back.

When I finished work the next day she was gone, and her stuff as well. Dad kept coming over when he noticed I had women visiting and flirted with them. The majority of these women told me that he was pressuring them for sex saying, "You want a real man… come to my apartment".

I was really looking for some kind of direction again from my parents but again Dad just wanted my girlfriends and Mom wanted my money.

I soon started treating the women visiting me rudely, as I was drinking too heavily. I missed out on some pretty good prospects. I had several women chasing me and to lose one now and then didn't bother me. When I was drunk one evening Dad convinced me to send a woman I was tired of his way. I got slapped by her for mentioning this.

"Your dad is a dirty old man," she said, and walked out the door with tears in her eyes.

Cara and I dated once in a while to see if we could work it out again, but it didn't feel right any longer. I think she just might have wanted to get back together. She did ask me one evening while lying in my bed if I'd buy Ashley and her a couch.

I started laughing. "Crap, that's one of the things you didn't take."

She just giggled as she rubbed my chest.

I got up the next day and she had left the model number of the couch she wanted and the name of the store on my kitchen counter.

I had that couch delivered two days later for her and Ashley.

Cara came over on the weekends once in a while to have a drink or two. When Dad knew she was coming over he made excuses to visit and flirt with her. He wanted Cara badly, almost obsessively, and finally I wouldn't let him in my house if she was there.

I had decided that the single life was for me. When I wanted the company of a woman I'd just call her and she'd come over and be gone the next day. I had lots of money, no one to tell me what to do, and peace and quiet whenever I wanted.

My job, though, started taking a hit; I had a hard time getting up on time in the morning.

I don't know how many times the owner called me into his office, "You were late again today. Get here on time."

I didn't care anymore and worked fewer hours every day.

I was ready to quit, then I hurt my knee and went on workers' compensation from Labor and Industries. I had knee surgery and collected checks for nine months.

It was party time for me and I started drinking more and more. One evening one of my girlfriends and I went on a motorcycle ride to the waterfront. We drank just a pint of tequila and it made me really tipsy. I told her I couldn't drive my motorcycle and she said, "Yes, let's go home and have fun."

I started the motorcycle up, she climbed on the back and we took off towards my house.

I saw a police car start to follow me and then he turned on his light.

I said, "Crap! I am going to get a DUI!"

She hugged me and said, "Hit it!" so I did.

We were in a ninety-mile-per-hour run from the law. I whizzed in and out of traffic and almost got away. All I had to do was swing to the left lane, cut in front of the van in front of me and we were gone. The van would have blocked the police car and I'd be out of there. I knew they had my license plate but I thought, *I'll deal with it tomorrow.*

I took a sharp cut to the left lane and hit the curb at ninety.

I don't know how long I was out but when I woke up the ambulance was there and the paramedics were asking me questions.

I asked, "How is the woman who was on the back of my bike?"

They said, "A little road rash, but she'll make it."

She had been wearing a full-face helmet and I had given her my jacket. I was just wearing a light cotton button-up shirt and got quite a lot of road rash. My helmet saved my life as it had broken and had pieces of mulch in it. I broke my wrist and had to have a few stitches in my arm. Overall we came out of it really well.

At the hospital they drew blood to check my alcohol level. It was .23 and the officer said as I lay in the emergency room bed, "If she had died, I'd be taking you down for vehicular homicide."

He wrote me a few tickets and, after the hospital staff was done putting me back together, let me go home.

I was in front of the courtroom about a month later and a police officer walked up to me.

"Do you remember me?" he asked.

I said, "No, sorry."

He said, "You're sure looking better. I'm the officer you tried to outrun."

"Sorry," I said and he replied, "I sure got in a lot of trouble because of you. My sergeant yelled at me for not bringing you in for a DUI."

I asked, "Why didn't you?"

"It looked as though you had lost enough that night," he answered.

I shook his hand, went into the courtroom and was fined $548.

I tried to put my motorcycle back together but it just wouldn't run right again so I sold it. I also knew that if I bought another motorcycle I would kill myself so I only drove my S-10 Blazer.

While I was laid up in my house for a couple of weeks healing, I got a phone call from one of my friends, Rena. She offered to make me dinner at her place. I was feeling better so I drove to her apartment and sat on her balcony as she cooked.

I had taken Mary, a woman who lived right across from Rena's apartment, out for drinks a month earlier. There was a little friction between us but I paid no attention to it. We had gone to a lounge and were having a great time. Mary was a pretty gal with a lovely smile, long brown hair, freckles and a nice body. We laughed, played a little darts and flirted with each other suggestively.

I was ready to take her home when I noticed three guys making eyes at her across from us. Mary smiled back at them and did a bit of flirting, too. I didn't care because I was taking her home and it was kind of cute.

Mary asked me if we could leave and wanted to know if I could stay over. I told her yes and got up to pay the tab.

When the bill was settled I turned around to see where Mary was. She was talking to the three guys, so I waited for a few minutes about twenty feet away. Then a couple walked by me and the woman said, loudly enough for me to hear, "He must not care."

I looked at her and said, "Yes, I do," and started walking towards Mary and the three guys.

They looked at me as if to say, "What are you going to do, three against one?"

I walked up to the middle one, the biggest, and chest-shoved him to the floor.

I grabbed Mary's hand and said, "Ready to go?"

The guy got up and said, "Let's go outside."

I said, "You first."

The couple that had instigated it were watching as we walked outside.

The three guys lined up across from me and the one I had chest-shoved said, "Now what you going to do?"

I took one step toward him and chest-shoved him again, putting him on the ground.

I looked at the other two, who were just standing there, and said, "Come on, punks!"

One of them said, "Come on, it's not worth it."

I said, "You don't want any!"

They helped their buddy up, quickly got into their car and sped off.

I told Mary to get in my Blazer. "We're going to your place."

I drove her home and the whole time she was rubbing all over me. "No man has ever done that for me before. I want you," she said.

I stopped in front of her apartment and said, "See you later." She looked shocked and walked to her door alone. I didn't really care that I had to fight for her but when I fight I like it on my terms. She looked back as she went in her door and I sped off.

I knew at that time I had a "death wish" and didn't care about anything.

When I was sitting at Rena's waiting for dinner I noticed a woman carrying in boxes to another apartment right across from Mary's.

She noticed me, too, and asked, "You have a Phillips screwdriver I can borrow?"

I said, "Yes, in my Blazer. I'll bring it to you in a bit."

I waited for about ten minutes and then told Rena, "I'll be back in ten minutes."

She said, "Dinner's almost ready."

I left anyway and grabbed the screwdriver. I knocked on the other woman's door. She opened it, and I asked what her name was.

"Theresa," she said.

I asked what she needed the screwdriver for. "To change my vacuum cleaner belt," she answered.

She was friendly enough and had a pretty nice body on her. I, of course, said, "I'll change it."

While I was changing the belt, she kept leaning over and showing me her cleavage. Then she offered me a drink.

I said, "Sure," and she asked about the girl that I was with.

I told her I was visiting and we were "just friends."

I went back to Rena's about an hour later to eat dinner and we got into an argument. "I'm cooking you dinner and you spend your time over there!"

I put my plate down and headed back to Theresa's. She and I had a few drinks and I spent the night there.

After that Theresa and I spent more and more time together. Then she asked me to move in. I thought about it and figured we could make it work.

I had also found a drinking partner; Theresa drank as often as I did. We always laughed together, had great sex and I thought I could be loyal to her. I moved in with her and her two young kids about three months later.

CHAPTER 15

PARTY TIME AND MY SECOND MARRIAGE - THANKS, DAD

I can honestly say that Theresa and I had a great couple of months together. Barry and I were now working as steelworkers on the same job and making good money. Theresa was watching a couple of kids during the day so money was plentiful. We shared laughs together and the great sex made us both happy.

Theresa liked the "bad boy" image that I had. I didn't care much about anything, even living. I had bought a Glock 9mm, 15 shots in the clip, and always carried it with me. I had my concealed weapons' permit and usually tucked my Glock in my inside coat pocket.

One Halloween night we had Theresa's kids out in Tacoma. We parked my S-10 on the corner and walked her kids around the block so they could trick or treat. While I was waiting on the sidewalk a car went speeding by and I yelled, "Slow it down!"

I continued walking house to house with the kids and Theresa. When the kids finished that block I started across the street to get my Blazer. Halfway there I noticed the car that I had yelled at parked behind mine.

Then I spotted four Black guys sitting in the car, staring at me. One started opening the car door and without missing a step I slid my hand inside my leather coat. They closed their car door and I got in my rig. I looked back in

my rear-view mirror and saw one of the passengers place a
hand gun on their dashboard. I pulled mine out, loaded
one in the chamber, and placed it in my lap. They started
up their car and the passenger took his hand gun off of
the dashboard. They backed up enough to pull into the
street and slowly started coming past me. I quickly rolled
my window down and placed my Glock just below the
window. I knew I had fifteen shots, and I was ready to rock
and roll with them.

I lifted my Glock up just as we were door to door and
I saw they had their hand gun pointed at me. I was almost
ready to start firing when they pulled their gun down and
sped off. I'm sure that I would have been a drive-by victim,
but since I had firepower, too, they didn't want a fair fight.

Theresa and the kids saw what was going on from the
other side of the street. Theresa kept bragging all the way
home that finally, "I have someone not afraid to protect
us."

The kids were happy, too. They had bags full of candy.

It took me a while to stop Theresa from provoking
fights when we went out. She almost got me killed a few
times, usually by Black people.

I usually went to Reno for a few days once a year and
asked Theresa, "Want to go on a trip with me to Reno?"

She said, "Yes" and we got a sitter for the next weekend.

We were having a great time there and I had won a few
hundred dollars. We got really drunk together and she
mentioned marriage. I was so drunk that I said, "Let's go"
and we hailed down a taxi.

I had no intentions of marrying her when I left home,
but when we arrived back in Washington she was wearing
a wedding ring. I wanted to get an annulment but finally
thought, "What the heck, Theresa is a good woman."
Married life wasn't that bad and I started getting used to
it.

All good things come to an end, though. I had made up my mind that I was going to be loyal to Theresa. Then it happened - we were sitting at the pool and the pool man walked by. Theresa was in her bikini and she spread her legs at him. I saw him smile and she closed her legs.

I asked, "What was that about?"

Theresa didn't answer and soon we left the pool area. We went home and she got a phone call. When she got off the phone she asked, "Can I go out with the girls tonight?"

I didn't think too much about it and said, "Sure, honey, anything you want. I'll watch the kids."

Theresa put on some very seductive clothes that night before going out and I just said, "Go knock them dead. You're hot!"

I kissed her off for the evening and slapped her butt on her way out the door.

I noticed that she walked through the parking lot instead of going to her car. Her girlfriends weren't there but I just blew it off. We were in love, right? Nothing to worry about, I thought.

When Theresa wasn't home by three in the morning, I started to worry: car accident, stranded somewhere, too much to drink, and is she at her girlfriends'?

No, Rena told me the next morning that Theresa was with the pool man that night. I just couldn't believe it; I was completely loyal to her. But the next day I was told by several people that Rena was telling the truth.

The next Friday night Theresa asked me to watch her kids again. "Sure," I said and I knew where she was going - out with the pool man.

When she left I asked the woman downstairs from us, "Will you watch the kids? I'll give you twenty bucks."

She said, "Yes," and I took the kids to her apartment.

I got dressed up and knocked on Mary's door. "You want to party?"

I had ignored her up to this point because of what she had pulled on our previous date.

Mary said, "Can my girlfriend go with us?"

I replied, "The more the merrier."

Mary said, "Come back in an hour and Tracie and I'll be ready."

An hour later I knocked on the door and Tracie answered. *Damn!* I thought as I checked her out from head to toe. She smiled and I knew it was going to be a nice evening. She was wearing a nice blouse that showed her cleavage and a mini-skirt with heels. I walked inside and saw Mary standing there wearing almost the same outfit. These gals were hot to trot and ready to party.

I walked them to my Blazer and we were off.

They both sat across from me at our booth and I was trying to decide which one I wanted for the night. I couldn't make a decision so I chose them both.

Tracie said, "Those guys over there keep staring at me. It makes me nervous."

I said, "Don't worry about it."

I got up, walked to the guys and said, "Quit with the gals. They're mine for the night."

I had my leather jacket unzipped and they could see my Glock in my inside pocket. They got up, paid their check and left without saying a word.

Mary said to Tracie, "Don't worry. We're in safe hands."

Tracie stood up and sat next to me. She began rubbing my thigh and Mary was running her foot up and down my leg. We had a few more drinks and were having a great time. Then the girls excused themselves and went to the ladies' room.

They returned a few minutes later, sat down and Mary said, "We're ready to leave. Do you wanna party with both of us at my place?"

I looked at Tracie and she said, "Let's go!"

I paid the bill and we went back to Mary's place.

Mary went straight into her bedroom and turned down the covers. Tracie led me into the bedroom and we started undressing. I knew this was going to be a great night.

And then it happened.

I had been the last to come through the door and hadn't locked it behind me. Suddenly it swung open and there stood Theresa.

I told her to leave and go back to her pool man. She wouldn't leave and I had to drag her out of there.

I slept on our couch for the next week or so.

We tried to work it out but our monogamous relationship had already been broken. Theresa stopped seeing the pool man and I just worked and came home. I would see Mary now and then but Theresa had her eagleeye on me so we could never hook up.

I took off work one day and met Tracie at a lounge and we ended up getting a motel room. I slept with Tracie to get back at Theresa for sleeping with the pool man. Tracie wanted to continue our affair but I had gotten even with Theresa and we went our separate ways.

Barry and I had kept in contact and he invited us to a house party, Curt and Debbie's, friends of his. We got a babysitter for the kids and met Barry and Kathryn there. Curt and Debbie were a fun couple and we had a few cocktails. Curt mentioned that they had a three bedroom house for rent about a mile up the road and we went to check it out. We needed a larger place and a new start so we took it.

We moved from the apartment to the three-bedroom house the following month so Theresa and I could start fresh. Starting over fresh was not as easy as it sounded, though, and I resented going home. I started hanging out with Barry and over at Curt and Debbie's home.

Dad started coming over when I was working and I could tell he was interested in Theresa. I blew it off as his fantasy and didn't think for a moment that Theresa would fall for his advances.

We were struggling a bit at the house with only me working and found it hard to pay the bills. Dad mentioned that there was a place available next to him in the quadruplex where he lived. I couldn't get Theresa to go to work so we decided after quite a few months to take it for less rent.

I had slowed my drinking to almost a halt but Theresa couldn't stop. I'd come home from work and she would be passed out in the bed or on the couch. She became physical at times and I had to fend her off. It came to a point that she would force me to slap her to stop her from hitting me. She broke stuff during the day and left cigarette burns on the furniture and carpet.

I found vodka bottles hidden all over the place. I'd put my bathrobe on and there would be one in my pocket, or I'd go to the cabinet to get a box of cereal and a bottle would be hidden behind it. I would just pour it out and replace it with water. I quit giving her money and took her off my bank account.

I couldn't figure out how she was still buying booze.

Then I noticed she and Dad gone at the same time. Theresa would say she was going to the store and in about five minutes I'd see Dad leaving the parking lot.

It all came to a boil when I told Theresa I was going to the store. Instead I went to Dad's place and parked around the corner. She called him while I was there and asked him to come over. I heard this and knocked on my door, as if I was him.

She opened the door expecting Dad and stood there wearing only my open robe with a shocked look on her face.

I slapped her across the face and walked away. The cops were there before I could take off and I was arrested for assault.

The first night Dad and Theresa slept together was that night. It continued for I don't know how many times. I just couldn't believe it was happening and when I questioned Dad he lied, "She is my daughter. I wouldn't do that to you."

I wanted to believe him but still, in the back of my mind, I knew something was going on.

When I got out of jail I called my sister Connie and asked her to find me a place in Eugene, Oregon, where she lived. She agreed and one week later I quit my job. I wasn't going to take Theresa or her kids with me. She kept telling me nothing was going on with her and Dad and I wanted to believe her so I changed my mind at the very last moment. We packed up the U-Haul and all went to Eugene and our new apartment.

Two days after moving to Eugene Theresa confessed that she *had* had sex with Dad. I shut down mentally and went into a depression.

Kenny, Connie's ex-husband, lived in Eugene, too, and we talked about moving Theresa out. I wanted her to leave but at the same time I didn't want to be alone. Kenny would come over now and then and we'd go out.

One night we brought a couple of women back to my place and started partying a little. I hadn't seen Theresa for a week or so and figured she was gone. It was that night that she decided to call and one of the women answered the phone.

Apparently she had been out with her guy friend at the same bar we were and was sitting in the back so I didn't see them.

Theresa scared the two women off with her phone call and came home a half hour later totally blitzed from alcohol.

She told me, "I was at the lounge and the guy I was with told me, "Don't worry if he sees us. I have a gun in my ankle holster."

She went on to say that he had no problem about shooting me. I carried my pistol after that just about everywhere I went. I wasn't sure why he would defend her from me but I wasn't going to let him take me out without a fight.

Kenny and I went out to that lounge another time to have a few. We were sitting up at the bar with the dancing floor to my left. The tables were also to my left and I noticed a pretty woman sitting at one of them. She was staring at me and got my attention. I tried to ignore her but every time I glanced that way, she was looking at me and giving me a nice smile. I tipped my drink at her and she tipped hers back to me. I noticed her getting up after that and walking my way. She smiled as she walked by and did a bit of butt shaking.

She went into the ladies' room. I waited for her to come out, and as she walked by me she ran her fingers across my back. I tapped her on her butt and turned to talk to Kenny.

When I turned back to look at her I saw a rather large, muscular woman coming toward me. She had a pack of cigarettes rolled up in her t-shirt. I thought, *Holy moly!* and wondered why she was coming my way.

She came within a foot of me and said, "You touched my woman's ass."

I started laughing and said, "Sorry."

She was looking for a fight and I wasn't going to be the one to beat up a woman. She was so upset that I don't know if I could have beaten her, but I certainly wasn't going to find out.

I looked at the woman who had started all of this and said, "Thanks a lot!"

She said, "Sorry. I'll be here tomorrow night alone."

I sucked down my drink and said, "No thanks," and decided to leave for the evening.

Theresa wasn't at home much of the time and truly I didn't want her there. I got up each morning around nine and got myself a cup of coffee. Around ten o'clock every morning I saw a blind woman walking down the sidewalk getting her exercise. I always wanted to go talk to her but I didn't want to startle her either. She walked back and forth using her white cane.

We were there for about three months and all I did was drink, becoming more and more isolated. I went up to Washington State one weekend, and got back my .25 caliber pistol that I had loaned my ex-wife and I planned to *shoot Dad* but couldn't find him. I stopped by a few of my friends' homes pretty much as a good-bye tour.

When I returned back to Eugene the kids had been sent to their dad's place in Spokane and Theresa was passed out on the floor. I went to bed and tried to figure out how I was going to kill myself.

I woke up in the middle of the night with Theresa's back up against mine. I was shaking and sweating at the same time, and it felt like it was 30 degrees in the apartment. I opened my eyes and noticed two people standing in my bedroom doorway. I focused my eyes and sat up on the side of the bed.

I saw a woman standing there holding the hand of a little girl about eight years old. They were dressed in 1800 southern dresses that fluffed out from the waist down. They just stood there for what seemed like ten minutes.

Finally, without moving my lips, I asked them what they wanted.

"Don't worry, Dave. You'll be with us soon."

Their mouths didn't move. I just heard them say it. I started to stand and they slowly vanished.

I contemplated what they had said for several days and every night hoped they would come back and explain themselves, but they didn't.

One morning at around seven or so I woke up and went into the kitchen. I finished a pint of vodka and waited until the liquor store opened up. Then I drove there and bought a fifth of vodka. I finished that around two in the afternoon and again drove to the liquor store. This time I bought a half gallon of vodka and started drinking that. I had finished about a third of it when Theresa and I really started arguing.

I called Dad and said, "I'm coming to kill you."

He said, "Shut up or I'll fuck your wife again." I slammed down the receiver and cursed him.

I walked up to Theresa and backhanded her across the face saying, "How dare you!"

She went to the phone and called the police.

I said, "SCREW THIS," and headed for my bedroom, grabbed my .25 pistol and went into the bathroom, locking the door behind me.

In a few minutes I heard a knock at the door and a voice saying, "Police."

I placed the gun to my right temple with my right hand. I stared directly into my own eyes in the mirror and watched a teardrop fall. I took a deep breath and closed my eyes.

I then said, "Please, God, forgive me and take care of Ashley," and pulled the trigger.

CHAPTER 16

SUDDENLY BLIND

When I awoke I wasn't sure if it was day or night. I wasn't sure where I was. But I knew I couldn't move my arms or legs. I later found out that they had me strapped to my bed. I felt a strong vibration on my legs and it was really dark. I had a bad headache and could only mumble.

I heard a soft voice say "Dave" a couple of times and I made a moaning sound. I couldn't open my mouth enough to talk so I just made whatever noise I could to acknowledge the person. I had no idea of where I was or what was going on, and no memory of why I was there.

As time went by I could hear more voices talking about me and I lay there in suspense, frightened as I have never been before. I must have dozed off and on for a while because of the medications. I woke up periodically with strange voices asking me how I felt. I just mumbled and moved my head for a yes or no answer. I felt comforted when a hand would squeeze mine when asking me questions.

I woke one time with someone holding my hand. It was a familiar voice but I didn't know who it was at first.

She asked, "Do you know who I am?"

I shook my head "no" and she said, "Theresa."

It took me a few minutes before I remembered she was my wife. I nodded my head "yes" to let her know I knew who she was.

As she held my hand she said, "You've had an accident and you're in the hospital."

I was nodding off and on so I am not sure of the time span. I woke again and heard Connie talking to me. I was beginning to be able to recognize familiar voices. Then I heard Mindy, Connie's friend, and Kenny, Connie's ex-husband.

I was starting to be able to speak a few words and I asked Kenny, "What happened?"

He wouldn't answer me.

The doctor was there and said, "Dave, you've lost a lot of weight. We need you to eat something."

I wasn't feeling very hungry so I refused to eat.

Mindy asked, "I have some butterscotch hard candy. Do you want one?"

I nodded my head "yes" and she put one in my mouth. The doctor again said, "Dave, you have to eat something."

Then Kenny said, "Dave, will you eat a Whopper with cheese? I'll go get you one."

I nodded my head "yes" and he went to get me one. I could only finish half of it but it sure tasted good. My doctor told me and also wrote on my chart, "Dave can eat whatever he wants."

I wasn't too much in a mood to care about that then, but it sure came in handy later.

I am not sure how many times this happened but it was pure pain every time. A nurse would come in and hold my head still and I had a God-awful pain. I found out later that they were changing the gauze in my head. A wound in the head has to heal from the inside out. Every time I would scream and yell, "Stop!" I finally found out the reason they were doing this was that I had taken a bullet to the head, in the temple.

One of the nurses massaged my feet with oils. Because my feet are so ticklish I would wiggle around like a fish out of water. I am sure it was comical and I am sure she was smiling.

I asked her once, "What are my legs vibrating for?"

She responded, "To make sure you don't get a blood clot."

The next memory was of Theresa telling me they were moving me to another hospital. I kept on telling her to turn on the lights but she never said a word and would change the subject. She later told me, "The doctor told me not to tell you. He wanted to be there."

One day the doctor came in my room with Theresa. He said, "Dave, you're blind. The lights *are* on."

I still hadn't regained enough sense to comprehend totally what he was telling me but every time I asked, he and the others kept reinforcing the fact that I was blind.

He went on to say again that they were transferring me to another hospital, Sacred Heart in Eugene. I was being moved out of critical care and into rehabilitation.

I heard the ambulance crew come into my room. As they started to put me on a gurney I said, "I need to have a bowel movement first," so they left the room and I tried to get up with Theresa's assistance. There was no way she could help me to the bathroom alone so she called for a nurse.

I was helped to my feet by the two of them and I whispered into Theresa's ear, "I don't want the nurse to see my penis."

The nurse started laughing and said, "Dave, don't you remember? We took a shower together a couple of days ago. I've already seen your penis."

I thought, *What the heck; if she's already seen it,* and went to the bathroom in front of them. Then the ambulance drivers came in again and transported me to another hospital. I later found out that I had been there for thirteen days: eight days in a coma and five days to get me stabilized in the Intensive Care Unit.

I don't remember the ambulance trip or much about the first week at Sacred Heart in Eugene. Later I heard that for several hours of the day I was strapped to a wooden chair in the hallway and was pretty much a zombie. I'm sure that they had medicated me very heavily and I was in another world. I recall that some of my family came to visit me while I was in my bed.

And now I had a roommate. I kept on hearing someone moaning really loudly and I asked the person to shut up. I was trying to hear whoever was talking to me but couldn't because of all the moaning.

I started yelling at the top of my lungs, "Make them shut up or get them out of here!"

Pretty quickly a nurse came running.

I kept yelling, "Get that freaking nutcase out of my room!"

Then I must have gone to sleep again because when I woke up I asked the nurse, "Who was here and when did they leave?"

She said, "Your mother and sister. They left a couple of hours ago."

I told her I wanted my own room and she said, "We moved him earlier and you have your own room now."

She asked me if I was hungry and I nodded my head "yes."

When she asked what I wanted I said, "What are my options?"

She replied, "Whatever you'll eat. What's your favorite food?"

I said, "What if you don't have it?"

"We'll make sure someone goes and gets it," she replied.

"Really?"

"Yes, Dave, whatever you want to eat."

Well, she had stimulated part of my brain to start working and I decided to test her sincerity. I said, "A cheeseburger with bacon and fries."

She said, "Okay. Give us about an hour."

I waited the hour. Then, sure enough, she brought me a cheeseburger with bacon and fries. It was made with all the fixings and she even brought me some milk and orange juice.

My hand-to-mouth coordination wasn't really working yet so the nurse helped me eat the burger. It sure tasted good.

She told me, "From now on anything you want to eat and at any time, day or night, just let us know. You have lost over forty-five pounds, down to 145 from 190, and we need to put it back on. You look like a skeleton."

I was glad she told me that. It helped me at least take a couple of extra bites when I felt full.

I still couldn't distinguish between reality and my dreams. In the first week that I was at Sacred Heart, I dreamed I was an "all-star" on the Cincinnati Reds baseball team and was going to play the next day in the all-star game. I was in a large room with all the other all-stars and had to go to the bathroom. I didn't want to wake up the other players, so I laid there too long and pooped my pants. For a while I didn't move, not wanting them to find out that another all-star had pooped his pants. Finally I got up slowly, trying not to make a noise, grabbed the poop out of my underwear and put it between the mattresses. Now I had it all over my hand, so I wiped it on my blankets and sheets. Phew! I had hid it from the rest of the players so no one would ever know. Now I wasn't going to be the laughing stock of the Major Leagues.

The male nurse who had to clean that up came to me the day I was leaving.

I told him, "I'm leaving today. Thanks for everything."

He said, "I had to clean your mess up," and wasn't very happy.

I said, "What mess?"

He told me about the poop between the mattresses and on my blankets.

I said, "That was real?"

He said, "Yes," and stomped away.

There were many other dreams that I thought were real as well: major earthquake, trapped inside a cow with a calf, partying with the doctor and his friends at his home, and my favorite – getting back to work.

In this dream all my heating and air installer friends came down to visit me. They had a job in Eugene and asked me to help them. They took me out of the hospital for the day and we went to install a furnace in someone's home. When we had completed the job they were getting ready to go back to Tacoma. I begged them to take me with them but they kept saying, "No, you have to sleep here tonight."

It was actually a nurse I was talking to and God bless her patience! When she laid me down to bed she probably went off to do her rounds. As far as I knew I was still at work and went back into my dream. My co-workers put a blanket on the homeowners' Corvette and laid me down to sleep. I woke up in the middle of the night because I was sleeping in a garage and cold.

I also had to go to the bathroom. One of my co-workers told me there were secret passages throughout the house. I saw a bookcase in the garage, got up and, sure enough, it swung open. I made my way through the secret passage and ended up in the master bedroom.

Only I wasn't in a garage. I was in another room of the hospital. Somehow I knew there was a woman sleeping there. I reached down to wake her and touched her shoulder. I think that some vision had come back as I remember the look on her face when she saw me.

She sat up quickly and started screaming. I quickly put one finger in front of my mouth and said,

"Shhh, I just need help finding the bathroom."

Soon I heard a nurse running in and saying, "He must be lost. Go back to sleep."

The nurse took me back to my room and helped me find my bathroom to relieve myself.

I still chuckle about that as I picture the woman waking up in the middle of the night and finding a strange man standing there. I still weighed only about 145 pounds, and was wearing white bikini briefs. I looked like a skeleton. As far as the woman knew, a ghost was in front of her.

For hours I laid in my bed wondering how I was shot in the head, trying to figure it out. I had all kinds of thoughts: did the guy with Theresa that night shoot me? Did I mess with the wrong guy's girlfriend? Did Dad do it? Or did Theresa do it?

After four weeks of being in the hospital I said to my doctor, "I want to know who shot me!"

I heard him pull a chair up to the bed and he sat down.

I said, "Who shot me?"

He replied, "You did."

"How do you know that?" I didn't believe him, and thought Theresa's boyfriend had done it.

I argued with the doctor for a while and he finally convinced me that I had done it.

I asked, "Why?"

After a brief pause he said, "I'll have your family talk to you about it."

He left and a counselor was in my room within five minutes saying, "Dave, do you want to talk? Are you okay?"

I asked, "How do they know I did this?"

The counselor said, "The police were there when you did it."

I asked her to leave so I could think and reassured her that I wouldn't try anything stupid. I had nurses coming in about every five minutes checking on me until they realized I wasn't going to hurt myself. They also had cameras on me watching every move I made.

I supposed I could live with myself if I did it with my own hand. But I still didn't know the reason why and I needed to know for sure.

My memory came back slowly and I started to remember everything - Theresa and Dad had betrayed me. All I could think about was that I had done this to myself over them and must have been drunk.

The next time I saw Theresa I told her I knew how and why I had gone blind. I asked her to leave and she didn't come back for quite a few days.

I needed Theresa to help me get out of the hospital so I pretended I didn't care about the past. That was really hard, especially when she kissed me or held my hand, but I had to hold my emotions in check.

My senses started coming back more and more every day. I credit this to two of the nurses, Margaret and Crystal. Margaret spent extra time with me helping with my motor skills and asking questions that made me think.

Crystal found out that I had a hard time remembering her name. Every day she worked she tracked me down and asked, "David, what's my name?"

I had a hard time, but after a while I could recall it. If it didn't come to me right away, I sat in my room until I could remember.

It was almost a week later after knowing what happened to me that my memory came back with clarity. I walked out of my room and Crystal said, "David, what's my name?"

I turned to her and said, "Crystal, I think I'm going to be okay."

Crystal gave me a hug and said, "I do, too."

The doctor kept telling me at every meeting, "You're going to need to go to an assisted-living center for about six months."

I kept on telling him, "No," and he started doing family interventions.

I knew that if I went to an assisted-living home I was never getting out. I must have gone through four family interventions. Each time I adamantly stood my ground saying, "No. I am going home!"

All I heard from my family was, "We can't take care of you."

I insisted, "I'll take care of myself!"

Throughout the next three weeks or so I stayed persistent. "I am going home."

The next two weeks in the mental ward I sat at the head of the table and often got messed with. I ordered what I wanted to eat; the other mental patients didn't like it.

The nurse came in around eight AM or so and I would put in my order for the day. I would order steak, burgers, fish and chips, pastas or chicken, and top it off with chocolate pudding or some other dessert. The rest of the patients got the regular hospital food and they always complained.

One guy threw his food and yelled, "Why do I have to eat this and he gets fish and chips?"

I responded, "Because I am Dave. Now sit down."

I was popular with the women in there because I shared my food with them.

Most of the patients there were "normal" people who had just forgotten to take their medication. They actually could perform pretty normally unless something drastic happened that they couldn't handle. This is when I began to feel more compassion for people with disabilities, more attuned to them.

One day my doctor asked me to follow him to a conference room. My family, wife and friends were there again. It was another intervention to get me to go to an assisted-living center.

I saw what was going on and immediately said, "I'm going home and that's all there is to it!"

The doctor said, "I'm transferring you upstairs to our rehabilitation floor tomorrow. If you can make lunch for me after five days I'll release you to go home."

I said, "Deal," and left for rehabilitation the next morning.

CHAPTER 17

BUILDING MY
NEW LIFE

I was moved up to my new room the next morning. When I reached the rehabilitation center on the fifth floor, I was introduced to Cindy, the Occupational Therapist who was going to teach me independent living skills. We walked around and she familiarized me with the kitchen area. They had an enclosed kitchen with all the appliances, food, cabinets and cooking utensils. They had stocked the cabinets with canned foods, coffee, breads and condiments.

Cindy told me straight up, "We have five days to prepare you for making lunch. That's it."

I told her, "No problem. I'll work as hard as I need to."

We started right then. She had me feel around in all the cabinets, the counter tops and the drawers with the silverware. We worked that first day for a few hours and I memorized where almost everything was; that was a drain on me. Then I ate lunch and took a nap.

I awoke a few hours later and started exploring the area using my white cane. I had only used the cane a few times and was bumping into everything. I was lost and couldn't find my way back to my room. An Occupational Therapist introduced himself and asked if he could do some experiments with me on my off hours.

I said, "Sure. Why not? Just come find me. I'm not going far."

He assisted me back to my room and I listened to the radio for the rest of the day. I didn't leave my room again that night; they brought dinner to me and I could find the restroom on my own.

The next morning my talking alarm clock went off at eight. I got up, got dressed and went out for breakfast. The food was good and I was starting to put the weight back on. Again I had no restrictions on how much food I could eat, so I ate as much as possible. I was feeling healthier, starting to laugh again and getting my brain back together.

Cindy came up to me after breakfast and asked if I was ready to go to work. I stood up and grabbed her arm for assistance.

Each day Cindy and I worked on independent living skills for the first few hours before lunch and then called it a day. She first taught me how to pour milk, butter bread and make coffee.

I ate lunch after that and then worked with the counselor who wanted to learn about blind people. He would move his hand around my body, stop it and ask me where his hand was. He kept it about six inches away from my body at all times. I was correct about ninety percent of the time. He told me that I was more attuned to that feeling than any other blind person he had worked with. I am not sure how I knew his hand was where I said it was, but there must be something to ESP.

He also took me swimming at the YMCA a couple of times and taught me a few things other blind people do for life skills.

Theresa usually came to visit around dinnertime and got a free meal. I could only smoke when she walked me downstairs because everyone who worked there wanted me to quit. That's about the only reason I wanted her there, and I couldn't care less if she came any other time. I would also need her to take me home when they released me. I found out Dad had been staying at my place with Theresa for a week or so while I was in the hospital so I just didn't care anymore.

Cindy and I kept working on my skills until the doctor showed up five days later. This was my day to prove myself with my newly learned skills. I knew that if I failed I was going to an assisted-living center and if I passed I was going home.

The doctor came into the kitchen and said "hello" to us. Then he asked Cindy, "Well, is Dave ready?"

Cindy responded, "I think so, but ask Dave."

I said, "What would you like for lunch, Doctor?"

He asked Cindy to leave. I was hoping she'd stay but this was part of my test. I heard his clipboard hit the table and he sat down.

I walked up to him and asked, "Are you hungry? What would you like for lunch?"

He responded, "I'm not picky. How about a sandwich and soup?"

I walked to the cabinets and grabbed a can of chicken noodle soup and the can opener. I took out a can of tuna fish, mayonaise and a couple of pieces of bread from the loaf. I then mixed up the tuna fish in a bowl and even cut up half a dill pickle to mix in. I put some water in with the soup and, while it was being microwaved, set up the doctor's placesetting, including a napkin.

I turned on the coffee pot and waited for the microwave to stop. Then when the soup was hot I got some crackers. I placed all of the food in front of him, one item at a time.

I sat down confidently and said, "Lunch is served. If you want coffee go get it yourself when it's done. You'd better eat it all, because I spent a lot of time making it."

He then stood up and told me his hand was out for me to shake and I shook his hand. Then he said, "You're released to go home tomorrow at six AM"

He opened the door and a minute later Cindy rushed in hugging me and saying, "You're going home, you're going home!"

She knew how badly I wanted to go home. Without her and everyone else helping to keep me alive, listening to all my dreams, the Commission for the Blind in Oregon and the nurses pushing me, I don't know where I would be today.

Before I left the next morning I found out that Cindy had watched the whole episode of me making lunch through a window in the hallway. I heard she had tears running down her face as she watched me.

I went to my room right after making the lunch and packed up my stuff. I was ready to go at three o'clock. That was a long day and night while I waited anxiously to leave.

I called Theresa and asked her to pick me up at six in the morning but got a strange feeling she wasn't overjoyed.

I waited until around six-thirty the next morning and called Theresa again. I asked, "Are you coming?" and she replied, "Oh, yes. I'm coming, oh, I'm coming!"

I knew she had a man there and they were in the middle of the act but I didn't care, I wanted to go home. I was leaving her anyway; just get me out of this hospital. I was in the hospital from April 12th to May 28th and all I wanted to do was go home. I was anxious to learn how to live blind and independently.

Theresa showed up at around eight o'clock and I was finally on my way home. I needed her for assistance at first but I knew it wasn't for long. She guided me up the stairs and opened our apartment door. I walked inside and, with the very first step I took, I banged my head into a bookshelf. I said, "Who put that there?"

She said, "I changed everything around to make it easier on you."

I said, "I remember where everything was before. Thanks a lot."

Theresa and I stayed away from all topics relating to Dad and the day of the shooting and I just tried to learn independent living skills.

Ashley came down to stay with me for the summer break and helped me a lot. She was only eight years old and it was extremely hard on her to go through this. I apologized to her over and over, asking her to forgive me.

Theresa and I were sitting across from each other one evening watching television. As she stared at the television, suddenly my sight came back! I slowly stood up and walked over to where she was sitting. She turned to look at me and I placed my hand right on her face.

I said, "I can see you."

I stood there holding her face until my sight went black again about five seconds later. That was the last time I ever saw anything again to this day.

I talked to my family and doctor the next day and they dismissed it as if it really hadn't happened. I know that it did though because how else could I have gotten up and walked seven feet across the room and put my hand directly on Theresa's face when she wasn't saying a word?

I only wish that Theresa wasn't my last glimpse of sight. I wish it could have been Ashley.

Theresa pretended she had a job and left during the day. One day my care provider was there and I asked her to go find my title to my S-10. She went into my room and came out a half hour later.

She said, "I can't find it but I think there is something else you should know."

I said, "What?"

She then decided that it wasn't her place to tell me.

I kept insisting, "I need to know."

A few minutes later she read me what she had found in my bedroom. She started to read off some notes that were left apparently after I had gone into the hospital. One said, "I'm sorry I have to leave as you're sleeping so soundly and so beautiful but I'll call you in the morning."

There were other ones but I can't remember what they said. I just grabbed my white cane and asked my care provider to take me to the apartment of the guy who had left the note. We argued about this for quite a few minutes before she assisted me to his apartment. I was furious and wanted to kick some ass and nobody was going to stop me.

We stood in front of his apartment door and I heard my care provider say, "You sure about this?

I just turned my head towards her and started pounding on the door. I knocked long enough that he knew I wasn't leaving.

After about a minute or so his girlfriend answered the door. I stood there stunned because I didn't know he had a girlfriend.

She said, "I know why you're here! My baby and I are leaving tomorrow morning for Kentucky and we're leaving this bastard."

I handed her the letters that he had left behind after the midnight visits with my wife. She read them silently and started crying.

The guy finally came to the door and slammed it on me, which made me more infuriated.

My care provider said, "We should leave. She looks like she got beat up last night and it looks like he might do it again."

This made me even madder and now I really wanted to kick his butt, but my care provider was able to convince me to go home.

At home I stewed for a half hour then said to my care provider, "Take me back down there!"

She insisted that I not go, but I demanded that she take me.

We ended up in front of their apartment door with me pounding on it again, wanting a fight.

"How dare you have sex with my wife while I was lying there dying!" I wanted to say to him.

I needed to punch someone and I didn't care if I got hurt or not.

His girlfriend came to the door after a couple of minutes and asked me to leave.

I told her, "I'm sorry, but not until he stops hitting on women and wants to meet me face to face."

I just couldn't handle my absolute fury about how he and Theresa had disrespected me while I was in the hospital.

It wasn't long before the police showed up. I felt a hand on my shoulder. Then the officer said, "Dave, let's go back to your apartment."

The police escorted me home, instructing me not to go back down there. I was turning the knob of my front door when Theresa drove up in my Blazer. There was silence when she shut the car door and slowly walked up the wooden stairs. I could hear every footstep. I'm sure my facial expressions told the police that they shouldn't leave. I was standing in the doorway with the police between Theresa and me.

"What's going on?" Theresa asked.

I just handed her the notes that her friend had left while I was in the hospital. I wanted to rip her throat out or kill something.

Then something, I don't know what it was, put a sense of calmness in me. Within one second I went from wanting to rip the heart out of my wife, to wanting to hold someone and just cry.

In the month that we lived together after my suicide attempt I found out that Theresa had been sleeping with three other guys, not including Dad, while I was hospitalized.

On July 1st I called my friend Debbie from Washington and said, "I got a U-Haul reserved. I need someone to drive it home to Washington."

Debbie said she would fly down and drive me back. She arrived the next evening and we picked up the U-Haul the following morning. Ashley, Debbie and I loaded the truck and were ready to go back to Washington.

I left Theresa my Blazer, some furniture, kitchen stuff and a few bucks for her to survive.

She tried to hug me as Debbie, Ashley and I got in the truck but I pulled away and said, "Have a good life."

CHAPTER 18

I'M NOT HERE TO BE TREATED LIKE A CHILD!

Debbie, Ashley and I were on our way back to Tacoma with a full truckload of my belongings. As Debbie was driving through Oregon the U-Haul's engine started rattling. The noise became louder so Debbie called the U-Haul company.

She was able to get hold of a customer service representative and said, "The engine sounds like it's going to blow. What do we do?"

The phone representative said, "Go to the next U-Haul station in Portland," and gave us directions.

It wasn't long before we heard a loud "bang." Debbie coasted to the side of the freeway. She called U-Haul back and told them where we were and asked for a mechanic to come look at the truck.

We sat there on the side of the freeway for a couple of hours, calling U-Haul over and over until Debbie's cell phone went dead.

A State patrol officer pulled up behind us and sat in his car for several hours, phoning U-Haul and giving them our location.

Most of the night went by and finally the officer said, "They know where you are. I can't stay any longer." Then he drove off.

By the time the sun began to rise we were all pretty thirsty. I had to take my prescriptions because I had a terrible headache, but we didn't have any water.

Ashley had a "water baby" – a realistic baby doll filled with water – that she loved and I mentioned there was water in it. But she went into hysterics and I gave up on the idea of drinking water out of her doll.

At this time of my life I was really angry and any little thing could set me off. I thought that I was mentally there but I hadn't fully recovered yet from my head trauma and acted like a fool sometimes, embarrassing Ashley.

I had had enough. I took off my shirt and got out of the U-Haul. Standing behind it I started flagging down cars for help.

Within a couple of minutes a truck with two guys in it stopped and offered us a ride. They dropped us off at the U-Haul station and the service representative sent a mechanic to look at the truck.

He radioed back that the engine was blown, and they transferred my belongings into another truck that day. We stayed at a motel overnight and picked up our new truck the next morning.

We finally drove into Tacoma and unloaded the U-Haul into a storage unit. We took Ashley back to Cara's and I went to Debbie's for about a week. We tried to start a relationship, but when she went to work I'd get a cab and go to the liquor store, which was about a mile away. Debbie wasn't having any of that so I went to live with Mom for a week or so.

Ashley stayed with me at Mom's and I'd make her walk me to the liquor store. She cried every time, and I felt really bad, but I needed to drink.

After about a week Mom and I started arguing about my drinking.

I called my best friend Jim and said, "Come get me. I need a place to live."

He was there in less than a half hour and I left.

I lived with Jim and his wife, Donna, for a couple of months, following the same routine. They would go to work and I'd get a cab to the liquor store. I was primarily there as a babysitter for their two young kids so they could go out at night.

I heard them arguing one night and went downstairs to their bedroom. Jim was getting physical with Donna and I told him to knock it off.

The next thing I knew Jim and I were fighting in his kitchen. We went at it for a while before he came to his senses and we stopped. He told me to get out and knew I had no place to go.

All I could do was call Dad. He came and picked me up.

I lived with Dad until Christmas Eve, when we had a big argument. I guess it made him feel better with me living there and cleared his conscience. He also supplied me with alcohol to keep me happy.

I felt really helpless because I could hardly do anything for myself. I couldn't leave the house without someone guiding me, I couldn't cook, and I didn't have any independent living skills. I was so bad off I was bumping into stuff even in the house.

I called up the Washington State Department of Blind Services and was transferred to a vocational rehabilitation counselor, Linda Wilder. We spoke for a little while and I made an appointment to see her.

When I arrived at my appointment I found her to have low vision as well. That intrigued me because I thought, *Blind people can work, too?*

Linda was very understanding and gracious. She was able to answer most of my questions and was very concerned about my drinking. I was honest with her and she was up-front with me. We filled out the paperwork for the application and I became her client. She recommended that I go to the Adult Blind School in Seattle where I could learn some skills for being blind. However she knew that I was drinking heavily and wanted me to go through rehabilitation first.

I rejected this in the beginning but knew it would be good for me. I finally checked myself into a three-week alcohol rehabilitation center and sobered up.

I quit drinking for about two weeks after my rehabilitation stay, but I couldn't handle the stress of being blind anymore so I started again. I was a full-blown alcoholic and just couldn't stop.

When I finished my alcohol rehabilitation I found a duplex and moved in with a female roommate I had met at the rehab center. I didn't think it would work out but I needed some company and someone to drive me around. She didn't have a car so I bought her a Camero to use and asked her to make payments to me. I also asked her to take me to places such as the shopping mall and fast food restaurants once in a while.

We were strictly platonic and I paid all the bills while she took care of the duplex. It wasn't long, though, before she started doing drugs. I wanted no part of them. I didn't think drinking was so bad but I'd never allow drugs in the duplex or around Ashley when she came over for visitation.

My roommate started bringing home guys and having them stay there when I was gone and my things began disappearing. She was always borrowing money from me and when I quit lending it to her she would bring her girlfriends over.

These friends were prostitutes and she told me if I gave her a certain amount of money I could sleep with them.

I always turned them down and it wasn't long before she was offering herself.

For more than two months she didn't make her car payments, so I repossessed my car and resold it. When she found out, she disappeared leaving all her belongings and never came back while I was there. When I did come home on the weekends, though, window screens were taken off the windows. I knew it was her and had Barry come over and fix the windows so they didn't open without removing a rod from the inside. I kept her belongings, mostly clothes, for about six months and finally gave everything of hers away to Curt and Debbie, my ex-landlords.

I was going to the Washington State Orientation and Training Center in Seattle. I lived there during the week and went home on the weekends.

The Training Center was a good place for me, because I was around other people who had lost most, if not all of their sight. I quickly hooked up with a blind woman and we started a relationship.

Over time the school taught me how to read Braille, cook blind and achieve mobility with my cane, as well as computer skills and woodshop. I also began to be more self-confident, which had me suspended from the school a couple of times.

I noticed right away that they wanted me to conform to their ways and never question them. I had always taken care of myself after my teenage troubles and I knew it would be difficult to live there.

Three housekeepers, one on duty at all times, were there twenty-four hours a day. There were up to sixteen students who lived there at a time. I was the "rebel" of us students and constantly argued with two of the three of the housekeepers. They were used to telling the students how far to jump and the students would jump. Not me, however. I'd tell *them* how far to jump and it didn't always go well for me.

I usually went home on the bus during the weekends to my place just to keep my sanity. I spent the last two months taking the bus from Tacoma to Seattle every day, a distance of 35 miles each way, transfering twice.

I lived by myself after losing my roommate and didn't have much help from anyone at first. I wanted it this way so I could learn to deal with my blindness and learn living skills. I cooked for myself by trial and error and burned a lot of meals. Pizza was a frequent dinner then and hamburgers if someone would get them for me. Most of the time I was on my own and I learned to take care of myself.

I didn't have much money after paying my rent, electric bills, and a taxi, and buying food. There were times when food was pretty scarce. I found it hard to ask family or friends for help as I needed to prove I could do it myself.

I did swallow my pride on one occasion and asked Mom to bring over her leftovers. She brought me some spaghetti and corn. I was so hungry that I wouldn't eat in front of her and when she left I ate it with my fingers. I didn't want to waste time getting a fork.

One evening in desperation I called Mom and told her I was starving. I asked if she'd take me to the food bank the next morning. That was one of the hardest things I did, and it hurt my pride to even ask. I explained that I didn't have money for a taxi and didn't know how to take the bus there yet.

"Please take me," I begged her.

She told me that she would be over the next day and get me some food.

We went to two different food banks and I was given enough to last until payday. I hated going to the food banks because I felt like I was begging, but I had no choice. I usually had to go by the 20th of the month as the food I bought would run out by then. If it wasn't for the food banks I don't know how I would have survived.

Mom had married a gentleman named Fritz about nine years earlier. He treated her real nice and brought stability to her life. I wasn't talking to my dad any longer and Fritz took over the role of father to me.

If I needed anything I'd call Fritz and he would usually get it to me within a day or two. If I needed it right then, he would drop what he was doing and come to my aid. Once in a while he would show up unexpectedly with a case of beer and we'd watch a ballgame or just sit around and tell jokes. I enjoyed this because most of my other friends before my attempt to kill myself acted like they didn't know me any longer.

Barry my old co-worker would visit once in a while if I called him and a couple times he left me money if I needed it. I also enjoyed Barry coming over as he would get me out and we'd have a couple drinks or he would take me to his house.

Curt and Debbie would also come over almost every other Friday or Saturday night to visit or take me to get something to eat. Curt would always come in and sit down and Debbie would head for my kitchen. Then I'd hear the water going in the sink and Debbie would wipe the counters down and do the dishes.

I looked forward to having friends come over and I'm sure it was tough for them to see me after what I had done. I wasn't a happy person either, as I still would go off in a rage for the smallest reasons.

I was really angry at Cara because she always huffed and puffed if I asked her to shop for Ashley and me. I would ask her when she was bringing Ashley over for my visitation to pick us up a hamburger or something on her way. I was always able to pay her when she arrived but she didn't have time to stop.

When Ashley was getting dropped off, there were a couple of times she drove us close to where we wanted to eat. Ashley didn't like this too much as we'd have to walk home. I wasn't aware of it at the time, but she was embarrassed to have anyone see her walking with me and my white cane. It got to the point that whenever she came over she insisted on taking a taxi wherever we went.

I could tell that my attempt at suicide really bothered Ashley. It bothered me, too, for her sake because now I wouldn't be able to protect her as well as she matured. I tried to reinforce the idea that I didn't do it to leave her, but that I was a complete mess and wished I hadn't done what I did. I apologized to her whenever I felt her being depressed. She'd hug me, but never forgave me to this day.

We did have some very good bonding times when Ashley came over. We used to cook together and it was a lot of laughs. I didn't know how to cook and Ashley was too young to know how. We made some pretty good meals together though; these were moments I'll never forget.

One night we were making a meatloaf and I asked her to get the crackers. She didn't say anything for a moment and then replied, "I ate all of them last night."

I just asked her to find something like crackers and she handed me a box of Honey Nut Cheerios. I thought it would work for filler, and it did. It actually gave the meatloaf a slight tang of honey and I've used Honey Nut Cheerios in my meatloaf ever since.

We did have some good times together.

One night I had a girlfriend over and we were all sitting there watching a werewolf movie. Ashley was next to me really close, and I could tell she was kind of scared. I liked playing practical jokes and excused myself to go to the bathroom. When I got up I went into my bedroom and grabbed my Halloween mask, which was a werewolf mask.

I went out the back door without them noticing and made it around to the front door. I knocked on the front door and I heard Ashley yelling for me to answer the door.

When I didn't reply my girlfriend asked who was there. I opened the door really quickly and ran inside with the mask on.

Ashley screamed at the top of her lungs for a few seconds and all I could do was laugh. I scared her pretty badly that night, and she ended up sleeping with me and my girlfriend.

I loved having Ashley there on the weekends but when she didn't come over I had to fend for myself.

There was a restaurant a few blocks away that eventually I was able to get to by myself. It wasn't easy going, though. The first time I mustered up the nerve and made it as far as the sidewalk. Then I turned back, terrified of getting lost, and called a taxi.

The next weekend I made it to the corner of my block before I had to turn around from fear.

The third time I made it about halfway to the restaurant and then I was turned in circles by a dog that was trying to bite me. I fought it off with my cane and eventually the owner called his dog inside. However I had lost all sense of where I was.

I heard a car driving by and I yelled, "Stop," as I waved my cane.

The car sped past me and I stood there in the street not knowing what I was going to do next. I could just imagine what that driver was thinking as I was coming towards him, yelling, "Stop," and acting like a crazy man. I would have sped up, too, and driven away as fast as I could.

However the car circled around the block and came back. I heard it as it came up to me slowly. A woman rolled down her window and asked if I needed help. I told her

I was lost and she drove her car to the curb. She offered to walk me home and I took her up on her kindness.

We talked while she guided me back home and she introduced herself as Rose. She lived only a block away and after that she often came over to check on me. She seemed to always be there if I needed anything and watched my place to make sure I was safe.

On my fourth attempt to get to the restaurant I set off early one Sunday morning. I rehearsed over and over in my mind my route to get there: go out my door to the sidewalk, turn left and go to the corner, cross two streets and take a right on the third corner. Once I got that far I realized that I could make it. I crossed a lighted intersection and had only about half a block to go. I was just about there and I felt really proud.

Then I heard a woman's voice, "Mister, Mister, Mister," and her voice grew louder every time she yelled.

She came running up to me and asked, "Where are you going?"

I answered, "Right there to Flying Boots to get breakfast."

She took me by the arm and said, "You're walking down the middle of the road. Hold on to me."

I could have figured that out on my own but it was early and there was no traffic yet.

I just laughed it off and said, "Thanks."

I had made it and I went in for a bite to eat. The waitress helped me to a booth and poured me some coffee. There were four guys sitting at a booth behind me and they sounded still drunk from the night before. They had seen me walking down the middle of the street through the windows and couldn't help making wisecracks about it.

I was just happy to have been able to get there and tried to ignore them. The waitress wasn't as amused as they were, though, and after a few minutes asked them to leave. They put up a scene but finally left. I appreciated what she had done for me and after that, whenever she worked on the weekends, I went there to eat.

I'd try to leave five dollars for a tip but she never accepted it and always gave it back, saying, "Buy your beautiful daughter a nice gift.

I soon found that I was traveling around pretty well - I had become a good cane traveler.

Every once in a while when I was crossing a lighted intersection some wise guy or gal found it hilarious to honk their horn when I was in front of their car. The first time it made me jump just about out of my shoes. The second incident I was a bit more prepared. They honked and laughed. I turned right at them and gave them the finger. I then gave them a few choice words and went on crossing the street. That actually was the last time that ever happened to me. I later turned that into a learning lesson at my college during a presentation.

Another time I was heading back from the grocery store and waiting for the light to change so I could cross. I was tapping my cane on the curb and all of a sudden it went out of my hand. I stood there wondering what had just happened. Then I realized it had gone into the gutter.

A man saw it happen and asked, "You need help?"

I asked if there was a way to get my cane back and he said, "No."

He took me to a tree and I picked out a branch and broke it off. Then I twisted all the little branches off of it and used it as a cane to get home.

I really felt sorry for a bike rider one day when I was at the same intersection. The light turned red so I could cross and I put my cane into the road to step off. The bike rider was going passed me and my cane went into his spokes. He went tumbling and crashed pretty hard. All I could do was ask him if he was okay and apologize.

He moaned, "My fault," then he walked away with his bicycle.

I can't count how many times my cane has been broken by cars taking a right turn when I had the cane out there. A lot of drivers are in such a hurry to take that right turn before a blind person might try to get across the street. I've noticed that most people are in such a hurry now that even waiting thirty seconds ruins their day.

I enjoyed the weekends but the weekdays at school were very long. I had a hard time going back on Mondays, but I knew I needed the skills from the Training Center.

It was a large building with nine or more rooms above a Lions' Club in the middle of a depressed area of Seattle.

Most of the students had secondary disabilities and half of them couldn't function "normally" on their own. Not to mention all the drama there; it just about made me more insane than I already was. I'm sure that I was a handful but then again they are trained professionals, right?

I felt very alone there and out of place. I tried to fit in but my depression wasn't going to let it happen. I would go to my room, put on my headphones and listen to my music. I also made telephone calls to ex-landlord Curt and had him come get me out of there for a couple of hours a few of the weekdays when my sanity was on the edge from dealing with people.

One evening I called my sister Barbara and during our conversation I mentioned I was craving no-bake cookies.

I went home that weekend and there was a package waiting for me. I opened it and found a tin canister that weighed a few pounds. When I reached inside I felt no-bake cookies filled to the top. I must have eaten half of them right then before I called Barbara.

"Thanks, Barbara, for the cookies," was the first thing I said to her.

We talked for about ten minutes and ended the phone call by saying "I love you" to each other.

I called my sisters whenever I felt really depressed and they always pulled me out of it.

A couple times I did smuggle alcohol into my room when coming back from my place on the weekends. I'm sure that didn't help with my adjusting to school.

We went on social outings once in a while with instructors to help us adjust to being blind. One trip I went on was a dinner and audio-described theatre play.

We went to dinner first and I filled up on chicken, pasta and veggies. We went to the theatre play next. I sat up front with my girlfriend and put on the headphones. There was a person describing the play so we could tell what was going on.

Once my belly is full I get tired. I was sitting in a comfortable chair and couldn't keep my eyes open. Soon I fell asleep.

The bad thing is that I snored loudly back then, and my girlfriend had to keep elbowing me. The actors had to go on performing while listening to my snoring.

The next morning we had a meeting with all of the people who had gone to the dinner and play.

When they asked for suggestions to make it better I said, "Don't feed a guy full of food and expect him not to fall asleep."

I was never invited on any field trips after that, but I wouldn't have gone anyway.

There was no way to have any fun in the dorm after classes. Most of the students were too afraid to be themselves and hid in their rooms. It was like a dead zone and nobody had a personality, so I thought I'd bring some life into the school.

One weekend I bought a squirt gun and took it to Braille class. I had a blind teacher so who could see me squirting students, right? Well, I thought it was a good idea. I squirted a woman while she was learning Braille and it got her book wet. I didn't think about it but it flattened out the Braille bumps and I had to buy her a new book.

I also got yelled at a few times by my mobility instructor for taking off at lighted intersections and almost getting hit by cars.

I told him, "They can see me. They better stop."

Quite often I just didn't care anymore. If a car had hit me I just hoped it would take me out.

But I would have hated to live through an accident and become even more disabled. I started to be more careful, thinking *being blind with no legs would be even more awful.*

I had an instructor named Jim and we didn't get along at all. He seemed to have a chip on his shoulder. But then again maybe it was the chip on *my* shoulder.

Near the end of my mobility training I was given homework to do. I was supposed to call the three businesses I was going to the next day and plan out my trip.

I went into Jim's office the next morning and told him I didn't have time to do it.

He stood up in my face and said, "You're going anyway! My intern will go with you!"

I wasn't going to let him put me down so I just shrugged my shoulders and said, "At least tell me what bus and what direction."

He told me, "The number five bus, north."

I immediately headed for the bus stop and his intern stayed ten steps behind me. The interns followed us near the end of our training and observed to see if we could get the route done without help.

I stepped on the bus, sat right across from the driver, and asked him, "Where is the postal station on thirty-second?" That was my first stop for my test.

I told him my dilemma and he chuckled, saying, "I'll stop the bus right in front of the door. Just go forward ten steps and you'll be there."

When the bus stopped I got off saying, "Thanks."

I went into the postal station and asked a customer for directions to my next location. The person gave me good directions and I entered my second stop without any help. I then asked someone for directions to my third location and traveled there with no mistakes. All the time the intern was following me and watching me. I asked a customer there for the location of the bus stop heading south. I headed that way. There was construction on the way there and a police officer asked me if I needed assistance.

I said, "Sure," and he took my arm. We were heading towards the bus stop when he noticed the bus was coming and we weren't going to make it in time. The officer waved down the bus, I jumped on and the intern missed it.

I chuckled all the way back thinking about him standing there waiting for the next bus.

I stepped off the bus at my stop and walked back a couple of blocks to school.

I was going down the hallway when Jim stopped me.

"So you didn't make all the stops," he said sarcastically.

I replied, "I made all three and your intern missed the bus back."

I was called into the office after lunch and had to sit there while they scolded me like a child.

I just sat there yawning, then said, "I did my route. Can I go now?"

I was passed that day for mobility and only had my cooking class to finish. The tradition was to invite five instructors and two students for a meal you prepared all by yourself. When you completed this test you were considered independent for cooking skills and passed the class.

They wanted me to set the table formally, cook the full-course meal, serve them and clean up.

I told them I would have a barbecue outside on a warm day and all of the students could enjoy the hamburgers and hotdogs I would cook.

I wasn't going to set any table or serve anyone and we'd use paper plates.

I wasn't about to have the instructors sit there and me pretend to like them. If I had had to do it, I would have made some potato salad, too, and left it out to spoil, hopefully making them all sick.

They passed me without me having to wait on them; they could make their own lunch as much as I cared.

During this time I found out that I was accepted at "Guide Dogs for the Blind" to get my dog guide. I was leaving for Oregon in two weeks. I had also been accepted into Pierce College, and one week after returning with my dog guide I would be starting my college education.

I did have a couple of funny times at the school for the blind, though with no help from the staff and students.

Ashley came to stay at the school for a week with me and went to class with me. She hated going on mobility lessons with me because I kept bumping into parked cars. That usually set off the car alarms; soon she walked far in front or behind me. I just laughed.

One time I was crossing a lighted intersection and there was a car partway into the crosswalk. I heard the transmission change gears, and the car backed up to let me pass. When I crossed the street and was on the sidewalk I heard a loud bang. The driver who had put his car in reverse had forgotten to put it in drive when the light changed to green. When he hit the gas he smashed into the car behind him.

I finished the school in ten months, on my thirty-third birthday. I walked out the doors of that school having quite a few blindness-related skills and never looked back.

A few years later they did away with the group living; now the students have their own apartments. The three housekeepers are gone now and I can only guess that the students are much better off learning to become more independent.

I flew to Portland, Oregon, two weeks later and the representative from the Dog Guide School picked me and a few other students up from the airport.

CHAPTER 19

TIME TO GET ON WITH THE REST OF MY LIFE

There were nine students in our class from around the country. We were shown to our rooms. Each of us had a roommate. Mine was a man from Kentucky and after hearing his voice I knew he wasn't from the Pacific

Northwest. I was a little worried from the way he talked that he might be gay.

I asked him right off if he had a girlfriend and he said, "Nope. I'm married with two kids."

I let out a sigh of relief but, just in case, I kept my distance and always made sure our shared bathroom was locked while I took my shower.

After settling into our rooms we all were shown around the campus.

It was a new campus; we were the second full training class. We had an entertainment room, a full-time nurse, a large campus, cafeteria and three square meals a day. This school was funded by donations and no students paid a dime for these services or dog guides.

For the first three days the trainers held the dog guide harnesses in their hands and had us give the commands: left, right, halt and forward. On the third day we were all sent to our rooms and told to wait for our dog guides. That was very exciting; not one of us students knew what we were going to get.

I preferred a bigger dog and received a yellow Lab named Clayton.

They left us alone for an hour or so in our rooms to bond with our dog guides and we just hugged and played. Then fun time was over and the work started.

I got up at six each morning and walked my dog guide. Then I took my shower and went to breakfast.

After breakfast we had obedience training with our dog guides and then got on the bus. They took us first to the student lounge, and we all took turns having our dog guides guide us around.

The first time I grabbed Clayton's harness I was a bit hesitant, not knowing if he would run me into something or run me into the street.

I built my nerve up to give the command to go forward. When I had mustered up the courage I said, "Clayton, forward."

Clayton took off like a bullet and just about ripped my shoulder off. I went with him and he took me right to the first corner without hitting anything. I almost fell into the street because Clayton stopped on a dime and I didn't.

My trainer said, "All I could see was your bright smile and you were booking."

It was nice going that fast because with my cane I walked really slowly and awkwardly.

We learned to trust our dog guides, and before long we were crossing busy intersections and going through malls and downtown areas with lots of people.

One thing most people think is that the dog guides take us where we want to go. It doesn't work that way; we have to tell the dog guide where to go. For example, we don't tell the dog guide to take us to Safeway. We have to know how to get there.

The dog guides will take us around obstacles and stop at curbs, stairways and any objects they can't get us around safely. When we get to a curb and the dog stops, we give a command to go forward, left or right. The dog guide doesn't tell us when the traffic is clear. We have to listen and give the command to go.

I was very happy with the training and the dog guide I received from Guide Dogs for the Blind and Clayton became my best friend.

After the four weeks of training we were taken to the Portland Airport and Clayton and I boarded the airplane. Dog guides go on the plane with us, not in the cargo hull.

The plane could seat upwards of 136 passengers but there were only eight tickets sold. I had the stewardess sit by me most of the flight, petting Clayton. She also had the drink cart in the aisle so I had a few. When we landed an hour later I could hardly walk. I learned at that moment Clayton would pull me in a straight line so I didn't wobble all over the place.

I didn't have anyone to pick me up so we took the airport shuttle home and finally pulled up to our duplex.

When we went in our front door I walked Clayton on his leash and showed him around. I went down on my knees to get to his eye level. I started making the "ruff, ruff, ruff" sound and Clayton let out a little bark. The dog guide school had taught him not to bark and he was a bit hesitant. When he let out his little bark I praised him and he let out a louder one. I let him loose from his leash and he took off, running through the house, barking. I wanted him to bark in case another dog was coming at us while outside or in case of some other kind of danger. It was so cool listening to him bark and just letting him know it was okay.

We went outside then and navigated our neighborhood, going to all the places within walking distance that I gone to in the past, and going three times faster. I soon learned that Clayton was an attention getter and lots of women wanted to pet him.

When I was using my cane, people would just get out of the way. It seemed as though they avoided me when they saw me coming. It was as if I had the plague and they didn't want to catch it. Often after purchasing an item from a store, the clerk would almost toss my change back. I'd hold out my hand and the clerk would drop the change, sometimes missing my hand so the change would fall on the counter or floor.

I'd roll my eyes as if to say, "Don't worry. You can't catch it." I even said it out loud a few times and walked away.

I learned really quickly that by just tweaking Clayton's harness a bit to the left or right he understood to take the next left or right. It got to the point that there were very few voice commands needed; we just flowed together. We had a few issues at first, though. Clayton wanted to bark at every dog, stop in the middle of a busy intersection and relieve himself, or get petted by everyone who made eye contact with him.

He put me through some really embarrassing times. A few times while we were crossing a busy intersection, he'd suddenly stop right in the middle of the street. I'd feel him hunker down and start going number two. When you're in the middle of the street and traffic is stopped, there isn't much you can do but wait until he's finished. I'd just stand there looking up at the sky and whistle. I knew everyone was watching and, of course, laughing. Hopefully I had a poop bag on me to pick it up. Then we would finish crossing the street and continue our trip. I'd laugh later, but at the time it didn't seem that funny.

One time Mom and I were going through a food court in the South Hill Mall in Puyallup, Washington, on Christmas Eve. The place was completely packed and we got separated. Then Clayton decided to squat and go number two. As I stood there everyone just stopped and it went quiet. There were hundreds of people there and I'm sure some of them couldn't finish their meals. That time I didn't have a poop bag and just had to leave it there. In the meantime Mom went to security and said to them, "My son is in here with his dog guide. Have you seen him recently?"

One of the security guards said to her, "He's down by the food court, and his dog left four cow piles."

I was kind of worried the next time we went to that mall and always made sure I had poop bags.

However, I dealt with it and we got along just fine. I also learned really quickly that when I left pizza on the coffee table to get a cup of coffee, the pizza won't be there when I get back. Clayton loved double pepperoni with cheese. It was his favorite.

We worked together for that first week and then it was time to really test Clayton. We had to go to our first day of class at Pierce Community College.

I was nervous and didn't know how well we would be received by the other students.

CHAPTER 20

BUILDING MY SELF-ESTEEM

My first day of college life was a bit intimidating. Kristi, an assistant from the Disabled Students Office, showed me to my classes. After each class she met me and Clayton and took us to the next one.

I noticed right away that we were going to be accepted and actually sort of became celebrities. I also noticed that Clayton was really a "chick magnet". I was single and I surely was going to take advantage of it. Everywhere we went we were stopped by women wanting to pet Clayton and asking my name. I had two dates the first week and loved school. My self-confidence grew immediately and I walked the campus with my head high. Everywhere we went we gathered a crowd – and it seemed that I was the prize to catch.

I was only thirty-four and single and I had my pick of several women. I dated for a while and finally let one of the women, Lisa, hook me.

Lisa had asked me one day to go home with her for lunch. She said she would feed me leftovers from the evening before. I had some time to kill so I went with her. She gave me some chicken and mashed potatoes, and offered me a drink. *Okay*, I thought, *food and alcohol. I'll keep her.*

She also had a really pleasant-sounding voice and, from what other guys were telling me, she had a nice figure. She was pretty cute and was single.

She would take me to the liquor store after school on the way to my place, stay awhile, then leave and go pick up her kids. This was our routine for a while; she was keeping me from dating other women.

I decided to get my associates' degree and Certification in Social Services and Mental Health. There was one problem, though. I fell in lust with two women and they both knew it. Susan was in most of my classes and I wanted to date her. She liked me but knew Lisa and I were seeing each other, although no commitment had been made yet.

One day Lisa gave me an ultimatum: "It's either her or me. Pick now."

I mulled it over in my mind for a day or so and then chose Lisa.

I now had made my choice; after two months we decided that I'd move in with her and her four kids.

It wasn't long before I knew I had made the wrong choice. Lisa cooked dinner only a couple more times and liked to spend all my money. Her four kids were good children but at the same time a handful. After she quit making dinners we ordered pizzas just about every night. Godfather's Pizza delivered and it was my favorite so I didn't complain too much. The couple times Lisa did cook it was awful, and I wondered who had cooked that first lunch she had fed me.

I lived with Lisa for a couple months and then decided to move out. The last straw was when she went out on Valentine's Day to a dance without me. I had to stay and watch her kids.

I did stop drinking except when we went out together, but before long Lisa drove me to drink again.

When I moved out, Lisa's brother helped us. When he walked into the garage he saw all the Godfather's Pizza boxes. She had just stacked them up there instead of throwing them away. He wanted to take them to the recycle station for cash.

I couldn't get out of Lisa's place fast enough. I moved into an apartment in Puyallup with Clayton, and Susan and I picked up from where we had left off.

I was new to Puyallup so I didn't know where the grocery stores or liquor stores were located. I called directory assistance; blind people usually get this service free. It's considered our phone book and an accommodation for our disability. I was happy to find out that there was a liquor store two blocks away and a Safeway three blocks. It was easy to learn Puyallup and the bus transit was convenient, too.

I took it really slowly with Susan because I respected her. We went out a few times but the fire quickly burned out for both of us.

I was doing well in school and had a 3.5 GPA. I had a friend, Don, who mentored me and tried to keep me in line. He knew I was drinking a lot and tried to help, but I was too far gone and in my own world. I should have been on anti-depressants because thoughts of suicide came up quite often.

In one of my classes I was required to give a presentation on any topic I chose. I decided to do it on blindness and cane travel. I purchased a boat air horn canister and was ready to give my presentation.

I went in front of the class and dimmed all the lights. I began by asking everyone to close their eyes. I had them picture that they were standing at a busy intersection wanting to cross the street. I gave a brief description of how to listen for cars stopping, waiting for the lights to change. I told them to picture the cars stopped so they could cross and to take a step into the street. As they were walking across the street totally blind they had to focus on getting to the corner before the light changed.

Then, as their eyes were closed and they were imagining walking across the street, I pulled the boat horn out of my pocket. I pressed the button for the horn to go off. The next thing I heard were desks tipping over. A couple of women even screamed.

I waited for everyone to pick themselves off the floor and compose themselves. Then I said, "Okay, that's some butthole blowing their car horn to see how far they can make you jump."

I apologized to everyone and went on with my speech. I had made my point but after class one guy wanted to fight me. I respectfully declined. I passed the class with a 3.2 GPA.

One time that Clayton and I *didn't* make any friends was in the computer lab. It was two days before the end of the quarter and final papers were due. I was writing my paper along with around ten other people at a long bank of computers. Everyone was typing away, trying to finish their final papers. As I was typing suddenly my computer lost its power.

I heard other students let out a moan and a few said, "What happened?"

The computer lab assistant came over to me and said, "Your dog must have shut off the power supply."

Clayton, shifting around under the table, had bumped into the power supply and hit the button. All the students who weren't frequently saving their work lost everything. All I could do was to apologize to everyone, and I quickly got up and left.

Most of the students controlled their anger towards me but a couple cursed me as I walked by them. All I could do was go to my next class and hope that they didn't lose too much of their work.

I only had a few classes left to graduate with my associates' degree, and I planned on going for my bachelors' degree. This is when I started the process of enrolling at the University of Washington-Tacoma. When checking my credits for enrollment I learned I still needed two classes of foreign language. I signed up to take two quarters of American Sign Language (ASL) at the Puyallup Pierce College Campus. I chose ASL so that down the road I could work with the blind/deaf population. I had my goal set on getting my rehabilitation degree and working with the blind population.

The first quarter of ASL went fine and I passed it with an "A". It was a little tougher than I thought but I got through it.

I had a tutor, Tony, sitting directly across from me signing and I felt his hands as he signed. This is called tactile learning. I also had a student, Shasta, volunteering to teach me and we met at my home several times.

The second quarter went well for the first half, until mid-term tests. I had prepared hard for this test, and before it started I was asked by the instructor to go wait in the hallway. I was the only blind student out of twenty-two and thought this request was reasonable. The instructor told me she would be out in about half an hour to give me the test.

I waited in the hallway and after about an hour she came out and told me she'd give it to me before the next class. I was told to come an hour early.

I waited before the next class, but she didn't show until class started. I asked her when she was going to give the test to me and she told me again to come early to the next class. I arrived an hour before the next class, and again she didn't present herself until class started.

I asked her again, "When am I going to take the test?"
My tutor also asked her and I was told by him that
I wasn't going to take it. In protest I didn't show up at
the next class. During the class that I didn't attend the
instructor pointed at my empty seat and signed to the rest
of the class, "The blind man must be pouting because I
won't give him the test."

I attended the next class and was met in the hallway by
several of the students. They told me what the instructor
had signed to the class. She had also signed several other
insulting comments about me during class. They also told
me that they had gone to the foreign-language director
and complained.

I almost dropped out of the class, but I wouldn't
because I was starting the university the next quarter and
had to have the credit. I talked to the foreign-language
director a couple of times but he dismissed it.

I also learned the instructor would sign to the rest of
the class, "Look at the blind man trying to learn ASL," and
chuckle.

I spoke to everyone who would listen in the
administration, but nothing was done. I passed the class
without testing and as soon as my grade was posted I
hired a lawyer. The lawyer hired a private investigator
and we took depositions from all the students who would
cooperate.

My lawyer then filed a lawsuit against the instructor
and Pierce College.

In the next year and a half we took statements from
students, the instructor and several of the administration
personnel. A court date was set and I went on with my
education at the university.

I don't know how I did it but I was partying every night
and going to class the next day, and passing all my classes.

Susan came over and checked on me quite often, and she tried to change my ways but just couldn't. The last straw for her was on a night we were out together. We were standing in line outside a club when a former boyfriend of hers came up to us. I had met him before on one occasion and didn't like him. He called me the blind guy when he referred to me, and I took offense at being called that.

When he walked up to us I had been drinking already and he put me in an instant bad mood. I reached out with both hands and grabbed his shirt. Before I knew it we were wrestling on the ground.

Fortunately it was broken up really quickly. I didn't know it until I grabbed him but he was a pretty big guy. We stood there toe to toe and all of a sudden I felt him kick me between my legs. I couldn't see it coming, of course, and it doubled me over. I immediately stood right back up and reached out, grabbing a shirt.

The next words I heard were, "Police!" and I let go quickly.

I told the officer that I was blind and didn't mean to touch him. He understood and I asked him to call me a cab. He did and I left Susan there with another female friend of hers.

Susan and I talked at school a few more times in passing but that ended our chances of building any kind of relationship.

Barry my old co-worker or Curt and Debbie came over a lot to get me out of my apartment and we would go party at Curt and Debbie's or go out to the clubs.

I was trying to get it together but as soon as I had a few shots I'd get my "badge of courage" and act stupid. I was a nuisance at my apartment, keeping my music loud whenever I was drinking.

One day an old-sounding man I didn't know banged on my screen door and said, "Turn that shit down."

I yelled back at him, "Screw you," and turned it up louder.

Little did I know he was my future father-in-law.

The man and his wife, Jackie, lived two doors to the right of me and their daughter, Carmen, lived three doors down on the left.

It was my thirty-fifth birthday and Ashley was with me.

The two of us left my apartment and headed toward the liquor store. On our way out of the building Carmen and her fiancé stopped us and I told her it was my birthday.

She said, "Come over when you get back and have a drink."

Ashley and I hurried to the liquor store and on the way there I asked her, "What's she look like?"

Ashley said, "*Dad*, why do you always ask me that?"

I asked again and she said, "Blonde hair, thin and pretty."

When we got back from the liquor store I had a few drinks with them and went home.

The next day I went down to the pool with my dog Clayton, and Carmen was there with her mother Jackie. We talked a bit more and she played with Clayton.

I had Kate, one of my "friends-with-benefits," over a couple of days later and there was a knock at the door. She answered the door wearing my bathrobe and Carmen asked me to come outside.

Carmen was drunk. "You want to go to the park with me?" she asked.

I said, "Give me five minutes and I'll come down to your place."

I went inside and told Kate she had to leave. She protested but eventually left. I went to Carmen's apartment and we headed to the park with Clayton. It was a rainy day and we sat in her car drinking alcohol.

It wasn't long before she asked me, "You can't see anything?" with a giggle.

I said, "No."

I had a feeling she was exposing her breast. I reached over and, sure enough, grabbed a naked breast.

We had our fun in the car right there in the park. Then we got dressed and Carmen took me and Clayton about a block away from the apartments and dropped us off.

"I'll call you in a couple days," she said before driving off. "I had fun."

When Carmen's fiancé came home, he noticed Clayton's dog hair in her car and confronted her. She broke off the engagement that night and kicked him out.

That wasn't the end of the two people we were seeing, though.

Gary, the guy Carmen was going to marry, and Kate, the gal I was seeing, got together. They would go over to my neighbor's place and cry on each other's shoulders.

Gary still had a key to Carmen's apartment. One time he hid in the shower and then jumped out at her, scaring her. She changed her door locks after that and he just hung out at the neighbor's house with Kate.

Kate wasn't so easy to get rid of, though. On several occasions she chased Carmen around town in her car until Carmen could lose her. One time she slashed Carmen's tires and I had to buy four new ones.

Kate would also wait for Carmen to go to work and then stalk me. She stood in front of my screen door and just stared at me. When you're blind you still have that sense that someone is looking at you, but you can't see who is there.

Once I found a cut near the lock on my screen door, so I called the police because I thought Kate had made her way into my apartment. They were only a block away and they arrived quickly and searched my apartment. But she wasn't in there.

I received a phone call about a half hour later and it was Kate.

"How are you?" she asked.

I answered, "Fine. Please don't call here again."

Kate said, "I was looking through your door at you and I left quickly when the police showed up. They saw me standing there but I walked right past them and left."

Then she asked if she could come over and talk.

I said, "Five minutes and that's all."

Kate showed up within one minute and I let her in. She had been drinking and it wasn't long before she got physical with me for turning her down. I called the police again and she left within two minutes.

When the police arrived one of the officers said, "We arrested her for a DUI and she'll spend the night in jail."

I didn't want that to happen but now it was out of my hands.

The next day when I was walking to the store I heard a car pull up at the side of the street. A car door closed and I heard Kate call out my name.

I stopped and asked her to please leave me alone.

She gave me a hug and we didn't see each other again until the day of her DUI court date. I was called as a witness but didn't have to testify.

Gary had also quit bothering us, and Carmen and I started our relationship. I thought it was going to just be us two in the relationship, but I also had Jackie and Carmen's father, Farrell, to deal with.

CHAPTER 21

MARRIAGE NUMBER THREE AND NICKOLAS

Carmen and I had enough money because she worked and I had money coming in from Social Security Disability and school grants. We had a lot of fun going out and we both loved to drink. Farrell loved to drink, too, and hung around with us at our apartment. At first it was fun listening to his war stories but after a while these got old.

Carmen and I were in love.

Then one day she said to me, "I'm pregnant."

I was overjoyed with the thought of having another baby and we moved into her apartment together. I was going to school at the time, finishing up my associates' degree, and she worked at a Ross store as an assistant manager. Clayton, of course, loved Carmen, too, because now he was fed table scraps.

I didn't know it but I was now with the woman who I would later compare to Dad's ex-wife, Helen.

Ashley and Carmen were getting along really great when Ashley stayed over on weekends. The two of them went shopping a lot and even Carmen's mom Jackie participated with them. Farrell usually came over after they left and wanted me to get a bottle. Carmen and I had slowed down on the drinking when we found out she was pregnant, but Farrell wanted me to keep it up because I was his source when Jackie wouldn't get him any.

One day I asked Jackie to go with me to the jewelry store in February to get Carmen a promise ring, and I walked out of there with a wedding set after Jackie convinced me it was a good idea.

I thought that Jackie and Farrell wanted us to get married, but I found out later that Jackie told Carmen, "It's the right thing to do even though it's just temporary."

It wasn't long before I knew Jackie and Farrell were living their lives through Carmen. They had a son in prison for murdering Jackie's aunt and they didn't want to fail twice as parents.

Carmen and I flew to Reno, Nevada, in March and we were married.

We moved into a house one block away from Jackie and Farrell's new condo. The two of them couldn't help from meddling in everything we did. If Carmen and I were discussing something, Carmen had to get their approval before agreeing to it. In their eyes I was wrong in everything I did, and they started tearing Carmen and me slowly apart.

Farrell would come over drunk and start arguing with me over the littlest things. Once he had to crawl back home through the schoolyard because he was so drunk. We went over there for dinner sometimes and Jackie would have a bib on him because he spilled food all over himself. Jackie and Carmen put up with him and dismissed it as a mental condition he had from lack of oxygen a few years earlier.

Farrell and I didn't talk for over a year one time because I made a joke and he didn't like it.

In August, 1998, Nickolas was born, my first and only son. I was so proud I wanted to tell Dad but I couldn't muster up the nerve to do it. I called Mom and she showed as much interest as getting stung by a bumblebee. Barbara showed the most enthusiasm and even sent Nickolas a blanket that she had made with her own hands.

Ashley was in the delivery room when Nickolas was born and I hoped it would build a brother-sister bond.

It backfired on me, though. Ashley's mother Cara told her, maliciously "Your dad has always wanted a son. Now he won't love you anymore."

When Carmen and I heard this we tried to let Ashley know it wasn't true and we both loved her as much as Nickolas. But Ashley started to rebel and soon there was a major rift between her and Carmen.

Carmen and I wanted to try to repair this rift. I planned a vacation to Montana for a couple of weeks, both to get away from my in-laws, Jackie and her husband Farrell, and to have Carmen and Ashley mend fences. Connie's daughter, Christiana, flew up to visit us and we took her with us to Montana. Ashley and Christiana were only one year apart and got along well.

But Carmen blew that the first day traveling to Montana with her negative attitude towards both girls.

The whole time was miserable for both Ashley and Christiana because of Carmen's jealousy. We ended up flying Ashley back to Washington and Christiana went by car to Mom's. I tried to stop it before it went that far but I was like Dad and let them handle it. Of course that put a big rift between my sister Connie and me, and she wouldn't talk to me for many years.

We came back to Washington a week later and then it happened.

Carmen got drunk and called up one of her past boyfriends. She took off and I watched Nickolas.

Around two in the morning I got a call from the old boyfriend. "She's too drunk to drive," he said. "I put her to bed. She'll be staying with me tonight."

I took care of Nickolas that night and when she came home the next morning I asked her, "Screw him?"

She was still half drunk and said something to the effect of, "Yes, so what."

Carmen and I should have split at that point, but I loved Nickolas so much I couldn't leave. We hardly slept in the same bed for the rest of our marriage. Whoever went to sleep last got the couch. The only time we had sex was when Carmen got so drunk that she woke me up after I had gone to bed.

I started seeing other women and Carmen did her own thing.

I was now attending the University of Washington working on my bachelors' degree. One day in early December I was standing outside after class with Clayton, waiting for my bus.

From out of the blue a man asked me, "How are you doing?"

I answered back with, "Fine, what are you up to?"

"Do you know who I am?"

I thought it was one of the librarians from the UWT library and said, "Ron."

He said, "No, it's your dad."

I was a bit shocked because we hadn't talked for about five years, and then I just said, "Hello. How have you been?"

We chatted for a while and I showed him a picture of Nickolas and Carmen. He got a little choked up and then asked me if I wanted a ride home.

I thought about it for a few seconds and then said, "No, I'll take the bus."

He said, "okay," and walked away. I stood there wishing I had said "yes" so we could talk more, but I didn't want him knowing where I lived.

I had mixed emotions about how I felt about letting Dad back into my life. After discussing it with Carmen, I decided against it.

Later that week he drove up to me again as I waited for the bus and asked me again if I wanted a ride.

I said, "No, thanks," and he drove away.

On January 30, 2001, my sister Barbara called me and said, "Dad died today from a heart attack."

Dad and I only had that short conversation just three weeks earlier, but I'm glad we had that time before he passed.

When Barbara and I finished talking I called the coroner and he told me, "His heart blew up. He died before he hit the ground."

I knew that he had died of a broken heart and, from what Jim told me, he was tired of life.

Carmen and I went to Dad's apartment and met the owner there. Dad had tried to make it outside and died on his porch, possibly attempting to get help.

I had Clayton with us when Carmen, Nickolas and I went into his apartment. I knew that he had kept some of my belongings from when I had lived with him five years earlier. I had asked him about them right after I left but he denied having my tools, VCR and a few other items. I guess he figured I didn't need them anymore because I was blind. I found them in his apartment and finally got my stuff back. Even today I find that I have stuff missing all the time. When I talk to other blind or low–vision people, most say they experience the same from so-called friends and family.

When I was going through some of Dad's belongings I kept feeling a really chilly air slightly blowing on me. It could have been that I was really spooked but I knew his spirit was still there.

Carmen and Nickolas were in the kitchen when I heard Clayton start growling. Carmen, in a scared voice, asked me to come quickly.

I walked into the living room and she said, "Clayton is growling at the door and his hair is up on his neck. I looked outside and nobody's there."

That is exactly where Dad had been found earlier that day. Now I was really spooked and headed back into his bedroom. I sat on his bed and felt around for the telephone on his nightstand. Finding it, I placed my hand on the receiver to pick it up. I didn't know it but Nickolas had followed me in there and when I was picking up the receiver he laid his hand on mine.

I just about jumped out of my skin as he said, "Hi, Daddy."

I had to get out of there that very second. I picked Nickolas up and waited outside. I kept telling Carmen, "Let's go. We'll come back tomorrow."

She took her sweet time but finally we left in the brand new car that Dad had bought just three months earlier. We went back a couple more times when Barbara flew up from California, but I left almost everything there for the owner to give away.

Luckily Dad had made all his arrangements before he died and we only needed to attend his funeral. He was cremated and had a military burial at the Tahoma National Cemetery in Kent, Washington. I was given his flag and the soldiers gave him a twenty-one-gun salute. The Air Force did this free of charge because of his twenty years of military service and I wanted this for him. I previously ask the funeral home to set it up and they said it would be $765 extra. I didn't know how we would pay for it. I then called McChord Air Force Base and asked them how much they would charge us.

They said, "No charge."

I told them the funeral home was going to charge us and they said, "They'll just call us and keep your money."

The Air Force did a tremendous ceremony for Dad, and I'm sure if he was watching he was very proud.

To this day I wish that I had let him give me that ride home. Maybe we could have patched things up before he died. When I heard about his death, I went to my knees and asked God, "Please forgive him and let him into heaven."

I could have used some of his advice because life away from school was getting pretty rough. We had a man in his early twenties who was mentally challenged and blind living with us. Carmen took care of him as his care provider and made pretty good money for it.

He loved Carmen but hated me because I had rules. One was that he not touch my dinner plate if I wasn't home. This young man would eat until he got sick, so when I returned home all the dinner was gone. He was a good man but for some reason he loved to irritate me. I attribute some of it to his mental condition, but not all.

He soon fell in love with Carmen and wanted me out of the picture.

After about two years of this I had him removed from our home by the police. He threw a tantrum and destroyed his bedroom again, for about the fifth time. An ambulance came and picked him up. After a seventy-two-hour psychology examination at the hospital, he went directly into a group home. Carmen blamed losing her job on me, but I was looking out for the safety of Nickolas, who was only three years old.

It was about this time that Carmen started drinking again. One evening she was driving Ashley and a friend to the skating rink and she didn't make it back.

I got a call from Ashley saying, "Carmen is in jail for drinking and driving and I'm with my mom."

Carmen lost her driver's license for a year and was fined pretty heavily. This made it tough as now we had nobody in the house who could drive. Typically, Carmen's parents blamed me for Carmen drinking and driving. It didn't surprise me when I heard what they said, because everything bad that happened was my fault in their eyes. I was in my last year of earning my bachelors' degree, and I knew I'd have to get Carmen and Nickolas away from Carmen's parents for us to have even a chance of keeping the marriage together.

CHAPTER 22

SHOULD I STAY OR SHOULD I GO?

I started the University of Washington-Tacoma (UWT) in April of 1999 to earn my bachelor's degree in inter-disciplinary arts and sciences.

Linda Wilder purchased for me a new computer and provided me with my books on tape and other supplies: printing paper, text books, bus tokens, and other needed items. This was purchased with funds from the Washington State Services for the Blind, and I also leaned on her for personal support.

I took one class there – Third World Human and Civil Rights – and finished up my third quarter of American Sign Language at Pierce College. This was a pretty tough three months, traveling from one school to the other and working on my lawsuit.

I passed both classes, then I just had to focus on UWT. I had to spend a lot more time studying than most other students because all my books came on cassette tape. It was very time-consuming to find a certain page or area of the book.

I went into the Disabled Student Services Department and met one of the student assistants, Mardi Murdock. Mardi was about my age and we seemed to hit it off as friends. We could talk about almost anything and I trusted her. I had a crush on her but she always made me aware of where her boundaries were and that was in order to keep it professional. There was something in the way Mardi carried herself as a woman, and nothing seemed to rattle her.

I could always count on Mardi when I needed assistance. If she wasn't in class she'd drop anything she was doing and go to the library to help me research a topic, spellcheck my papers and, if needed, guide me to class. After a while she took some of the same classes and, if time permitted, we even studied together before the exams. She was instrumental in getting me through my first year, making sure I was aware of all my assignments and getting them in on time. I don't think I could have survived that year without her guidance and friendship.

In her last class before she graduated, we were in the same class. When the last test was over and it was about time for me to go to the next class I said, "Mardi, when you walk out of this classroom you'll be done. Are you sure you want it all to be over?"

Laughing, she walked to the classroom door and stood there for a split second. Then she jumped across the threshold and said, "I've worked hard for this degree. I'm out of here."

Mardi did very well after graduating. She went into the field of human resources and has had much success.

It was quite a transition for me after Mardi left and I was introduced to Anna. Anna was a bit younger then I was and she was very professional as well. We had the chance to talk about her son, who she loved very much, and sometimes I felt jealous of their relationship. I could always count on Anna, too, to help me out of a pinch. She made sure I had my books on tape before the quarter started, made time to ensure my tests were ready in my reading format, and took her job seriously for us students.

We did get into an argument one time and it got pretty loud. I was testing her on how far I could push her into doing my work. Anna quickly put me in my place.

I used all the services I was offered from the Disability Office. It was not easy going to the university blind, but I felt I needed to prove myself.

I do know one thing, I should have studied harder. I usually made a friend or two in class and we would discuss the material before and after class. I put a lot of my emphasis on the final paper to make up any low test scores that I might have received during the quarter.

When I did my presentation on Cuba in my Third World Human and Civil Rights course, I dressed as Fidel Castro and received an "A++."

I normally took a minimum of three classes per quarter and I kept pretty busy. When it came to crunch time at the end of the quarter I usually dictated my final paper to Carmen, because she could type a lot faster than I could.

I had another presentation to give in Environmental History, and I knew I would have to give it my all to pass my presentation. I rented a full costume of the Grim Reaper. I had the class wait in the hallway while I put the costume on, including skeleton hands, cloak, full face mask and skeleton feet, as well as a sickle. My assistant and I placed seven baby-food jars on the table, each one containing a different color of Kool-Aid. I also had a large, clear pitcher of water.

I stood there holding the pitcher of water as the students came into the room. They didn't know what was going on or who was inside the costume.

The room was buzzing for the next few minutes with excitement and then the professor said, "You can start your presentation."

I had my assistant slowly pour a small amount of Kool-Aid from each baby jar into my glass, one at a time. Then she named each bacterium, virus and so on that's in our drinking water. After she had named it, I shook the pitcher and it got dirtier looking. When all seven were in, I held it out and asked, "Anyone want a drink?"

The whole class was quiet and I took off the Grim Reaper face mask.

We then went into a question-and-answer period for a half hour and I had all the correct answers for the questions they could throw at me.

I felt really good about my presentation and left the classroom to a standing ovation.

My professor hunted me down later that day and told me, "You have just raised the bar on presentations at this university. Excellent job!"

I had to learn how to make up from areas that I was going to be short on. I wanted no less than "As" and "Bs"; this was very important for me. I knew I was being watched by the other students to see if I would get preferential treatment. I didn't, and I even out-performed half the other students who had no disability.

I was standing in the Student Affairs Office one day when I heard a woman ask for directions to the classroom for the Human Sexuality class.

I spoke up saying, "I'm in that class. Do you want to follow me?"

I'm sure when she looked at me with my dog guide she wondered how I was going to show her. But she said, "Sure," and I took her directly there. We went into the classroom and she sat right next to me. Little did I know it but I had just found a study partner.

Her name was Karen. She and I became close friends that quarter, discussing our home lives which were very similar. Karen's husband was cheating on her and my marriage with Carmen was hanging by a thread.

I hated going home except to see Nickolas, and I was getting screamed at by Carmen every time I turned around. Several times I'd sit down for a meal and wonder what was for dinner. I felt like a little kid with not being able to tell Carmen what I preferred to eat. The last time I put up with this was when she put some sort of stuffed green pepper on the table. Carmen knew I hated green peppers. I grabbed my plate and dumped it in the trash.

Carmen started screaming, "My dad told me you'll eat it or go hungry."

I went to the freezer and got some burritos to heat up for dinner that night.

After that Carmen got the message that I wasn't going to eat what my father-in-law Farrell thought I should but what *I* wanted.

When I was gone, Carmen and Farrell would get together on the phone or at our place and talk about me. Usually when I returned home from school or work Carmen was in a bad mood; Farrell had worked her into a frenzy about me and then left after having his drinks. Until the day Farrell passed away he controlled Carmen and she jumped at his every command.

My in-laws Jackie and Farrell were so involved in our lives that I couldn't scratch my butt without them knowing about it. Nickolas kept hearing from the three of them that I was a "bad daddy," but I was doing everything I could do to keep parenting him. It was no use, though, because when I went to school they would tell him the opposite of what I was trying to teach him.

Karen and I started meeting for lunch and flirted with each other all the time.

We were discussing our sex life one day and she said, "I have no sex life with my husband."

I told her that mine was non-existent as well.

She said that she was going to leave her husband. Then she asked, "Do you want to go get a motel room?"

I had to think about it for the rest of the day, but when we met after class I told her, "Meet me here tomorrow at noon and we'll go get a room."

I knew I was taking a big risk. If Carmen found out it would be the straw that broke the camel's back. But I didn't care anymore. I love Nickolas but even he was being slowly taken from me.

It wasn't long before I could tell Karen was falling in love with me and I was falling in love with her.

We would spend all of our available time together for several months. Then it happened.

Karen said, "I've left my husband and I want you to move in with me."

I knew I was in love with her because she was all I thought of night and day, but could I leave my son to be with Karen?

I spent most of my time trying to decide what to do and even lived for a week in a motel room while I attempted to make up my mind. Karen stayed with me during the day, and then she left during the night to take care of her children.

I had to make a decision and I made it when I called Nickolas.

He asked me when I was coming home. "I miss you," he said.

That was it; I packed my clothes up and took a cab home.

I left a piece of my heart there with Karen and tried to avoid her at school.

She knew I had made the choice for Nickolas but tried her very best to keep us close friends. I couldn't handle being alone with Karen anymore because she would start crying and I needed to stay with Nickolas.

I started doing internships off campus, one of which was at the Washington State School for the Blind in

Vancouver. I stayed there on campus for four weeks, only coming home on the weekends.

The school teaches kids from first grade through high school. They live on a beautiful, well-maintained campus through the week and either are bused or flown back home for the weekend. They have the same classes as public schools but all the students are blind or have low vision.

I was very impressed by the instructors' dedication to teaching academically and their encouragement of learning life skills.

On many days after the schoolday was over the school planned outings.

One outing that I attended with them was a snowmobile trip to Mt. St. Helens. The students had a blast and had many other experiences that they probably wouldn't have had otherwise.

In their living quarters they learned to prepare light meals, clean their rooms, and interact socially with students. They learned responsibility and some made money doing light jobs around the campus.

This school works very hard at preparing their students for life after graduation and entering adult careers or going on with their higher education.

The kids seemed to like it there, too, and most, if not all, were happy.

I attribute their success to the superintendent, Dr. Dean Stenehjem, and his professionalism.

I also completed an internship at the Division of Vocational Rehabilitation for eight weeks. Vocational Rehabilitation assists clients with disabilities starting at the age of eighteen up to retirement to assist in finding and maintaining employment. For example, they provide the computer equipment needed for a certain disability or provide higher education. This was a bit disheartening, though, because at this time they had very few funds to do anything. They had a three-year waiting list, except for the extremely disabled.

We made presentations at high schools and signed up teenagers who were going to graduate.

I heard many times, "Why should I sign up? You can't help me for at least three years." I found that situation to be difficult for the teenagers. I also got my first taste of how state services work from the inside, and I was impressed with the vocational counselors' dedication toward their clients.

It was around this time that my court date for my lawsuit came up. My lawyer, Carmen and I met for a mediation hearing the day before the case. We presented our evidence to the mediator and the State's Attorney.

We reached a monetary settlement after a couple of hours. The instructor was never going to work for the college again. We avoided trial and I walked out of there with a pretty nice check. I was also told that Pierce College had a new position for students with disabilities to address any concerns about possible discrimination.

I soon started thinking I could assist more people if I opened my own non-profit business.

I had taken a couple of classes of Non-Profit Studies and decided to get my certification. I knew there was going to be an annual national convention in San Antonio, Texas, that January. I wanted to attend and I helped do the fundraising for ten of us students at UWT to go. We held an auction and made enough for all of us to go. I packed for San Antonio when the day arrived, and flew down with a few of my schoolmates.

We landed in San Antonio in early January for the three-day conference. There were students there from all over the country and, of course, I was the only blind student and the only one with a dog guide.

I learned quite a bit from this conference and enjoyed mingling with other students from around the country. I also noticed that Texas wasn't that warm and I grew more interested in working for The Texas Commission for the Blind.

I graduated from UWT with a GPA a little over 3.0, and started putting in applications at the Texas Commission for the Blind for Vocational Rehabilitation Teacher positions. One afternoon I received a call from a regional director, Ron, for a phone interview. I answered all his questions and we arranged for my personal interview in Corpus Christi three weeks later.

Carmen and I discussed moving to Texas, and we decided to give our marriage one last try. My in-laws Jackie and Farrell were totally against it, though. They made that perfectly clear to me. Their attitude made me even more determined to have my family get away from them, so I flew to Corpus Christi for my interview. I really didn't feel that I had any ties left in Washington State, so why not?

I waited for about a month and finally received a call from Ron. He said, "I want you to start on the third of next month. Can you be here?"

I answered, "Yes," and started making arrangements to have our belongings packed and brought to Texas.

I also retired Clayton and he went to a family with four kids. Clayton had worked very well for me and it was his turn to just be a dog and play. In my experience dog guides should be retired after five or six years and enjoy the rest of their lives without having to work. Being on watch all the time, constantly working, takes a lot out of them.

I received three bids from moving companies and submitted them to Linda. The Washington State Services for the Blind would pay for my moving expenses one time if I found a job more than fifty miles away and needed to relocate.

They accepted the lowest bid and soon I left for Texas. Carmen and Nickolas stayed at Jackie and Farrell's house and were moving down in two months. I didn't know if they really would or not because Carmen was so influenced by her parents.

I took the airport shuttle to Sea-Tac Airport and boarded the plane.

CHAPTER 23

TEXAS

I landed in Victoria, Texas, in February 2003 – the day that the space shuttle blew up over Texas.

I had just arrived in a place that I had never been before, and I was very anxious to start my new job. On the flight I felt my luck was improving and really looked forward to a great new start. When I transferred planes in Houston to Victoria I was the only passenger except for a training class of stewardesses. I had six or eight of them waiting on me hand and foot. It was about a one-hour flight and each and every one of them took turns pampering me.

At the airport I had an airport employee call me a cab. I noticed nobody else was in the airport.

I asked her, "You the only one here?"

She answered, "Yes. This is a small airport."

We chatted for a while until my taxi arrived and I headed for La Quinta Inn. I found out during the ride that this was the only taxi service in Victoria and wondered how small the population was in this new city I now was moving to. I had always lived in larger cities, and I wasn't sure how the small city life was going to be for a blind person without my dog guide.

I checked in and a very nice hotel clerk helped me arrange my room for the month. When we finished putting my clothes away, I set up my alarm clock and laid down, quickly falling asleep after an exhausting day.

I woke up around four the next morning and turned on the news. It was already seventy-two degrees and I thought, *Well, I didn't need to bring my coats.*

I dressed in office attire and went to eat my breakfast. Then I called a cab to go to work, wondering how I was going to be accepted as "the new guy."

When I walked in I was greeted by the woman who would be my assistant. She seemed nice as she introduced me to the other six office staff. After the introductions I was led to my office, pointed to my desk and told, "Ron will be up from Corpus Christi in a couple of days to orientate you and do your final paperwork. Your computer is behind you. Ron said to read the manual and if you have any questions, call him." Then she left.

I got up to explore my new office. It was a nice big room, with adaptive aids scattered all over the place, such as talking watches, talking microwaves and magnifiers.

My six office peers included two vocational rehabilitation counselors, three rehabilitation assistants, and one child and family counselor. They all made their way to personally introduce themselves during those two days and took turns showing me around the whole office.

I was really missing Clayton for mobility and I'm sure I looked a bit awkward using my cane for the first time in several years. However I managed to get through it without hurting myself and grew more confident with the cane every day. Ron and his assistant came up as promised on Wednesday to finalize my paperwork. I put out my hand and we shook. Then he went off to talk to my other peers and his assistant came into my office. She stood in front of me and I put out my hand to greet her, the way I had greeted Ron.

My hand landed on her breast. As soon as I realized what had happened, I pulled back. But she just giggled and we went along with our business. I knew that I was as red as a tomato and thought, *Damn, they're going to fire me the first week for sexual harassment.*

The whole office shut down for lunch and we headed for a restaurant where I ordered fish and chips. I was the center of all the questions which wasn't good because, as I took a bite of fish, a piece got stuck between my two front teeth. I tried to work that piece of fish out using my tongue but it was jammed. I didn't want to pick it out with my fingernail, and if I decided I needed to go to the restroom to deal with it, someone would have to help me get there.

All I could do was answer questions with "yes" or "no" and shake my head. I'm sure they all wondered, *Doesn't this guy talk?*

Finally I was able to work the fish loose. What a relief that was; I could talk again without them seeing a chunk of fish dangling between my teeth. Back at the office I was told my duties as the vocational rehabilitation teacher and independent living specialist. My area was nine counties and my job was to travel to each of my consumers' homes and assist them in any skills and adaptive aids they needed to remain independent in their own homes.

I was to find my own driver, and the Commission would pay him minimum wage plus 35 cents a mile. I learned that my case load was more than 100 consumers and they hadn't had adequate services in many months.

I finished my first day reading up on my consumers' files, and then Ron, my regional director, offered me a ride to my hotel. He and his assistant Arora were staying there, too, for one evening and she helped me to my room.

She made it perfectly clear what room she was staying in and told me, "If you need or want anything, call me."

The next morning she knocked on my door and said, "Let's go have breakfast. Grab my arm."

As we walked to the restaurant I could tell she was a bit upset. "I was hoping you were going to call me last night," she said.

I replied, "I ordered pizza and ate in my room."

She started to say something else but I interrupted her. "I'm married," I told her.

She replied, "And so am I, but..."

I quickly changed the subject.

I woke up on Thursday morning and took a bus into work. I was on my own now and I began to set up my consumers to visit the next day. Then my assistant Ora walked into my office and closed the door behind her.

I turned to talk to her and before I could say a word, she said, "I've been working here for almost twenty years and if you screw with me I'll call the Equal Employment Opportunity Commission!"

I said, "What brought that on?"

She said, "Don't screw with me!" then opened the door and walked out.

I hadn't said anything inappropriate to her, so I knew I had an assistant with an attitude. I put it out of mind until a year later when she started more trouble.

I worked the rest of the day filling my next day's schedule and finding a driver to hire to take me around until Carmen arrived in April. The next day I went to my consumers' homes; I got back to the office around three in the afternoon. I was passing by one of the counselors' offices when he called me in.

I said, "What's up?"

He asked if I had seen a particular consumer.

I said, "Yes. I saw him today."

He then asked if I had given him a visual test.

I told him, "Yes, I handed him a large-print business card and asked him to read it."

He replied demeaningly, "I knew we should have hired a teacher with vision."

I was shocked at first, then said, "Tough. They hired me!"

I walked out of his office and went to mine. There I searched the consumer's case files. Nowhere was it written to give him a visual test. *Damn*, I thought, *I've entered a hornets' nest.*

I usually ordered pizza or burgers for dinner and ate breakfast at La Quinta. I generally had a drink or two after dinner.

I met a woman at the restaurant one evening. We got to be pretty good friends and talked on the telephone quite a bit. I was lonely and once in a while she'd come visit me in my room. I had no sexual interest in her; I just wanted conversation until Carmen and Nickolas arrived.

One night out of the blue she came over with a bottle of whiskey.

We had a few drinks, it was Friday, and she spent the night in a separate bed. I was so proud of myself because I didn't put the move on her and we remained only friends. We hung around together mostly for dinner at the lounge and she showed me around Victoria.

I made it through that month visiting and teaching my consumers and staying out of my co-workers' way until I went to Austin.

I arrived at the Criss Cole Center for the Adult Blind on March 1st and started my thirty days of blindfold training.

There were about five of us from around the state in the training class. When you were hired at the Commission for the Blind all new hires went through blindfold training. It was supposed to teach you how difficult it was to be blind, and to have empathy for our consumers. Even though I was totally blind, I still had to go through the training.

We took the classes just like the students there and then had the rest of the day off. I usually took a cab somewhere for dinner, because I was getting a *per diem* payment of $35 to eat. A couple of times I even had my dinner at the Yellow Rose, a strip bar, and had topless women dancing around me while I ate my food.

I stayed at the training center for three of the four weeks, and then I couldn't take it anymore. I checked into a hotel and waited for Carmen and Nickolas to arrive. They had left Washington by train, but the train got blocked by a derailment and they were running a couple of days late. They were finally flown in to Austin at Amtrak's expense.

I was waiting at the airport when they arrived. They didn't know I was coming.

I was sitting in front of a vending machine when I heard Nickolas say, "I'll take a bag of peanuts." They hadn't noticed me there.

I stood up, turned around and said, "Welcome to Texas."

Nickolas and I hugged and I gave him a wooden tool box I had made in the woodshop class.

I was surprised that they really were there because I knew Carmen's parents didn't want her to leave them. Jackie and Farrell had done their very best to convince her to stay in Washington, even trying to bribe her with a house and money.

When my training in Austin was completed, the three of us went back to Victoria and found a house to rent. We had a moving company bring our furnishings there and most of it arrived safely, but some was damaged or missing and we sued in small claims court and won a small percentage of the replacement cost to replace it.

We moved into a modest neighborhood and liked living there.

I hired Carmen as my driver and occasionally Nickolas came along for the long rides. My closest consumer was a one hour drive and the farthest was over two and a half hours away. When I went into the consumer's home, usually Carmen and Nickolas waited outside. Other times they came inside. Carmen got a check for working as well.

It just wasn't enough, though, and soon we were falling behind on our bills. Carmen loved to spend money that we didn't have and often left the checking account in the minus of hundreds of dollars before my check was deposited. I would bring home just a little over $1,600 a month, and one month the account before my deposit was made was overdrawn $800. It's pretty hard to live if half of your check goes towards overdrafts. Soon we were taking payday loans; we could never catch up.

Jackie and Farrell still had their noses in our business and it wasn't long before Carmen and I started drinking again.

We still weren't sleeping together in the same bed; Carmen usually slept with Nickolas on the couch or his bed. Every once in a while, though, she would get drunk after I went to bed and wake me up to have sex. When she was drunk and did that I could hardly stand it. The only way I could perform was to think about a different woman.

I kept truckin' along on my job, and I loved it. I was able to help my consumers continue to live more independently in their homes and purchase independent/living aids for them. I was known in my region as the "spender" and would purchase just about anything my consumers needed.

I supplied one of my consumers with a closed circuit TV one day and taught her how to use it. She told me that she wanted to live in an assisted-living center. She had a beautiful home and, because she had low vision, I tried to help her stay there. When I set it up, she was now able to fill her own syringes with diabetic insulin and almost started crying with joy.

I asked her to practice with it for a couple of hours and I'd come back. When I arrived back she was on her porch.

She walked towards me and asked, "Where did you come from?"

Smiling, I said, "Washington State."

As she hugged me she said, "No, you didn't. You came from heaven."

She took me inside and showed me how she had learned to paint her fingernails. I just laughed and said, "Now you can live in your own home."

She hugged me again. "Yes, I can," she replied.

This is the reason I worked as a teacher and stayed in my job for two years. I was able to help hundreds of people remain in their homes.

In the rehabilitation field you have the good and the bad counselors, just like any other field. I knew some counselors were not always looking out for their consumers, but only looking at the numbers. Much of the time counselors are graded on job performance by successful closures. One of the counselors in the Victoria office who is Hispanic would assist the Hispanic consumers and get the "white" consumers off their caseload as fast as possible, without very many services.

This particular counselor and I butted heads on almost every consumer we shared on each other's caseload. Several times I'd be in the middle of training and I'd go back and the case was "closed successfully." It was a big complaint with some of us teachers, and finally the "higher ups" made it so the counselors couldn't close the consumer file until the teacher services were completed. When this change was made it really allowed us teachers to provide better services.

I sometimes felt like an outsider while working there. I knew that because I was from the north I was looked at as a Yankee. I was even in a doctor's office one day getting a checkup and the doctor said sarcastically, "You're a Yankee, aren't you?"

I replied, "Nope. I'm a Seattle Mariners fan."

That made him a bit angry, so I got up and left.

I finally couldn't take the Victoria office anymore and transferred to Houston. It wasn't long before I found out Houston's office was just as hypercritical and I began to look for another job.

I had only one person I could talk to, Lucinda. She was the independent living specialist coordinator for the southern half of Texas. She was also an outsider and we just kind of clicked. We stayed in contact up to a couple of years ago, and she is the only reason I stayed in Texas for the time I did.

Carmen and Nickolas wanted to go back to Washington State and I was ready to leave Texas, too. I called up my old boss from the heating and air conditioning company where I had worked previously and he hired me as a telephone sales representative.

I knew that when we moved back to Washington the marriage would be over quickly. It wasn't much of a marriage anymore anyway and we only stayed together because of Nickolas.

I quit the Commission for the Blind and started making plans to move back up north. In late September we loaded a U-Haul and left Texas. It took us five days to get back to Washington, stopping along the way in Reno, Nevada, to do a little gambling. When we finally arrived in Fife, Washington, we stayed at a Motel 6. The first thing we did after getting up in the morning was to go to my in-laws', Jackie and Farrell's home. They weren't too thrilled to see me but Nickolas and Carmen had a nice reunion with them.

We stayed in Fife for a week or so and then moved to a Motel 6 near Everett, closer to my work. We hadn't brought our car up from Texas, so Carmen rented a car for a month at a time.

CHAPTER 24

BACK IN
THE RATTLERS' NEST

I went to work at Bob's Heating and Air Conditioning in Kirkland and Carmen found us an apartment a couple of weeks later. My duties were to call existing customers and sell duct cleaning and furnace maintenance on commission. I had never been into sales competitively before, and it was a real learning experience.

I discovered quickly that if you need to use the restroom you better get back fast. I don't know how many times someone would answer my phone while I was on a smoke break and transfer the call to their desk, taking my sale. I left almost a hundred voice mails daily and asked people to call back to schedule. It got to the point that I had to spend my first hour of work checking to see if any of the customers had scheduled appointments the previous evening.

Our sales manager, Ken, had his wife, Peggy, answering phones after hours. Peggy was well rehearsed at saying, "I'm sorry, I made a mistake, I'll fix it and give you your commission." There were times that Ken or my immediate supervisor, Lola, sneaked into my office area and watched me. They didn't announce themselves and they thought that I didn't know they were there. It's a bit unnerving realizing someone is staring at you who won't answer back if you let them know you're aware they're there. I'd just get up, go outside and take a cigarette break. Then I'd hear a door close as they left, going out the other door.

I knew it was going to be hard when on my first day Lola told me she was from Texas. I thought I had left my Texas problems behind. I was wrong. I did very well, though, for the first few months as long as they left me alone. But Lola was always coming up with new ideas that I knew wouldn't work. She just couldn't handle the fact that I was doing well without using her script, and Ken made excuses to downplay my great days of selling.

Ken and Lola were the talk of the office. She followed him around like a little puppy. I didn't care. I was making money. Why would it bother me what they did behind closed doors? It kept Lola out of my hair.

I tried several times to bring new ideas on creating more sales for myself and the others, but Ken and Lola always shot them down. The job was fun at first and I looked forward to going to work, but after a couple of months it got tiring listening to Ken and Lola.

I could only handle it if I ignored them and left early on occasion. I also felt bad selling customers services that they really didn't always need.

Carmen and I weren't doing well in our marriage and Nickolas could tell.

This is about the time that Carmen told me that Nickolas was asking her, "Why do I have to have a dad that's blind?"

Carmen and Nickolas were joined at the hip and Carmen was pitting him against me. There was something weird about how they interacted together. He was always by her side. If we went somewhere and someone asked him a question, Carmen always answered for him. He learned that she would do this so he seldom talked. Carmen homeschooled him after a brief stint in first grade, and he hardly got any interaction with other kids.

When I was at work Carmen confided in Nickolas about our marriage problems, and it wasn't long before he was disrespectful to me. It was as if I was walking on eggshells in my own home – at any moment Carmen would explode with anger towards me in front of Nickolas.

I would go to work and on quite a few occasions I'd get a call from Carmen saying, "I'm going to my parents for a few days with Nickolas." We hardly talked while she was gone and I really wasn't sure if she went there or not.

One day I was sitting at home by myself and I decided to call Karen. We set up a time to get together for lunch. She drove up to Everett the next day. At lunch she mentioned that she had money for a motel room, so off we went.

We started talking more and more with each other, but we both knew it was a "friends with benefits" relationship only. After a while Karen found another boyfriend and we stopped meeting.

I knew that Carmen and I were done; it was just a matter of time. I had serious thoughts about trying it with Karen and hoped she felt the same. It was just too hard on Nickolas seeing his mother and me arguing all the time.

Carmen's brother had been let out of prison and he was coming over quite a bit. He didn't care for me, and when he was visiting I left all of them alone. I didn't go down to Jackie and Farrell's place anymore, not even for holidays.

It was springtime and my commissions slowed down to almost nothing. I was making just enough to pay the bills and cover Carmen and Nickolas's health insurance. Carmen wasn't working and had no intention of finding a job. Money was getting really tight, but she kept on spending as if she was rich.

Then one day I came home from work and there were a couple of kids in our apartment. I overheard Carmen ordering Chinese food and heard the total of $57.

After she got off the phone I asked her, "Why did you order so much?"

She said, "We're feeding all the kids, too."

I said, "No, we're not. Have them go home and eat."

I called up the restaurant and cancelled the order. Then I sat on the loveseat and told her, "We can't afford it."

She came running from the kitchen and pounced on top of me screaming, "Don't tell me what to do!" She then, while we were screaming at each other, scratched my face with her fingernails.

I pushed her off of me and stood up, so she ran to the phone and called the police.

I became enraged and told her, "If I go to jail so will you."

I went outside on the balcony and waited for the police.

I was sitting outside smoking a cigarette when they got there. One female police officer talked to Carmen and the other officer, who was also a woman, came outside to talk to me.

She asked me, "What happened to your face?"

I said, "Nothing."

I knew one of us was going to jail and possibly both of us.

I said, "I ran into a wall."

The officers talked together for a few minutes, then one of them asked me to stand up. I did and put my hands behind my back. She handcuffed me and walked me past Nickolas down to her police car.

I spent the next three days in jail and was released with no bail on Monday morning. There were about thirty men and women getting arraigned that morning and no one but I was released with no bail. It was kind of sad listening to the women having thousands of dollars in bail and not being able to go take care of their children.

I received a public defender and was going to fight the charges of assault four, a misdemeanor.

Carmen convinced me not to fight it. She said, "Let's try to keep the family together."

I plead guilty and had to spend six days in jail, take anger management, and have an alcohol evaluation. Those six days were no fun. The other inmates were able to read books to kill the time, but all I could do was lie there and think. I also had a roommate who thought he was a vampire. He'd get up in the middle of the night and use his sheet like a vampire cloak. He would practice twirling it around and make strange noises. I wasn't getting any sleep so I requested a cell change and was moved that day.

One of the timekillers in jail was TV time. We were able to go to the TV room twice a day for about an hour or two.

One guy in there was totally convinced that his now-deceased father was the Green River Killer – a serial killer who had murdered many women in Washington. Listening to him made the time go fast and he had all of us laughing. He gave me some instant coffee and a couple of pieces of candy one day and I took them.

Then he said, "I own you now." The guy was serious.

I looked at him and said, "Get away from me, you queer, or I'll kick your ass!" He didn't bother me anymore.

I was finally released around five in the morning and Carmen picked me up. I took the risk of being arrested again because there was a one-year no-contact order. We went back to the apartment and I slept for the next day.

I really started to hate Carmen for doing this to me and we hardly talked. Then one evening I came home from a meeting and walked up to Nickolas as he was playing video games on TV.

I said, "Hey, buddy," and he said, "Hey, Dad."

Then a strange man said from behind me, "Hey, Dave."

I turned and asked, "Who are you? And where's my wife?"

He said, "Tim. Carmen's in the shower."

I went into the hallway and found the bathroom door wide open and Carmen in the shower. Tim had just come from that direction and I went into the bathroom to talk to Carmen.

When she realized I was there she quickly shut off the water and dried off. When she was getting out of the shower she stumbled and grabbed the towel rack, ripping it off the wall.

She was wasted and brushed past me in the nude. She went into the bedroom, got dressed and those two walked right by me, Carmen saying, "We're going to the casino."

I had the no-contact order on me so I didn't dare do anything to stop them; she would have just called the police again.

I fed Nickolas that night and put him to bed. He kept asking me, "Where's Mom?"

I just kept answering, "She'll be back later."

Carmen came in at around eight in the morning, half drunk. She lay there in bed saying she hadn't come home last night because she had been arrested for a DUI. She had spent the night in jail and was released that morning. The rental car had been impounded and now she couldn't rent another one. Then she slept for a couple of hours in a drunken stupor.

When she woke, she went across the playground at our apartment complex to Tim's apartment. For the next two days I only saw her a couple of times when she came back to check on Nickolas.

On Monday morning November 17, 2005 Carmen came into our bedroom where Nickolas and I were sleeping and threw a suitcase on the bed.

She said, "Get up. You're moving and I'm taking you to the bus stop."

I got up out of bed and grabbed my backpack and two suitcases and hugged Nickolas.

Carmen led me to Tim's car because hers was impounded. We put the suitcases in the trunk and she took me to downtown Seattle.

When I got out of the car I had two dollars and three cigarettes to my name. I asked Carmen for a few cigarettes and she gave me a couple. I stood there at the bus stop not knowing where I was heading, but I knew I was going to Tacoma.

As the bus pulled up, I turned to Carmen and said, "See ya."

She tried to kiss me and I just stepped onto the bus with my suitcases and backpack.

After I sat down I called Mom and asked her to pick me up at the bus station. I also called my grandmother and asked if I could stay there for a week or so. Mom picked me up and we headed for my grandma's.

I slept on the couch for a few evenings, trying to find a place to live. I tossed and turned most of the night thinking how nice it would be to get my hands around Carmen's neck and squeeze. I soon quit thinking that way, though, and focused on starting my new life.

It was a bit funny watching TV with Grandma because she had a nine o'clock bedtime. We'd be watching a movie and at exactly nine o'clock she'd get up with the movie half-over and shut it off. She'd kiss me good night and head for her bedroom. I'd just smile and wonder how the movie ended.

I called Karen and asked if she would mind me staying there for a while. She had a boyfriend but she spent most of her time over at his place. After a couple of days she called me and said, "You can sleep on my couch but I don't want my boyfriend knowing."

I agreed and took all my stuff to her place.

We flirted a lot but we didn't sleep with each other during those three weeks. I then began to look for an apartment and found one in Lakewood.

I had to put off moving in December as I paid the rent, bought food, and paid the bills for Nickolas to have a place to live in Everett. Carmen had my bankcard and had me overdrawn four hundred dollars that month.

I cancelled that bank account and had my check direct-deposited with only my name on it.

Once I settled into my own apartment I filed for divorce and custody of Nickolas. I also learned that Carmen and Nickolas had been evicted from their apartment. I finally found them through the post office. I soon found out Carmen had moved Tim into her new apartment and now all three lived together.

I finally took a one-bedroom apartment and moved in. I slept in a sleeping bag on the floor of my apartment and had a thirteen-inch TV given to me. I also had my old high school girlfriend, Debbie, give me some dishes and cookware, and then Karen, another old girlfriend, gave me blankets and furniture and within a month I was totally furnished.

I hoped to get some kind of relationship going with Karen again, but she was in love and I didn't want to come between her and her boyfriend. Once I had a bed, though, she spent the night on occasion. I was in love with Karen but I couldn't give her what she wanted so we remained friends, occasionally going out on dates.

I tried to stay in contact with Nickolas but Carmen made it very difficult. She was able to get a no-contact order on me by telling a bunch of lies that the judge believed. There was no way to check on Nickolas except through the occasional child-welfare check. That was the last straw for me; I was worried about Nickolas.

I was at my apartment with no way to get around because my cane skills weren't up to par. One day I was talking to a blind friend, Sue Burdyshaw. She urged me to get another dog guide and I finally called Guide Dogs of America in California. I filled out the application and was accepted. I arrived in California in April and had two weeks of intense training. The second day there I was given a male black Lab named Kosi.

We did a lot of hard work in those two weeks. The trainers were great and it seemed to go pretty quickly. I used to stay up playing Uno with a couple of women in the class and usually lost. It didn't matter, though, because I just played for the company.

One of the women, Linda, who was from Las Vegas, liked to go deep sea fishing. We made a pledge to go fishing together some day.

One day one of the students was missing for breakfast. She was a really heavy-set woman and not in very good health. It wasn't like her to miss a meal and I noticed her gone.

I asked, "Where's Mary?"

The nine students and the two trainers went silent. After a minute or so I said, "I'll go check on her."

I know what I was thinking and pretty much knew what they all were thinking, too. *Did she die last night?*

I went to her room and knocked on the door. I didn't hear anything so I knocked again, louder. Still there were no sounds coming from her room.

I went inside expecting to find her dead and said loudly, "Mary, are you okay?"

Finally I heard her say, "What?"

I said, "You're missing breakfast."

She rolled out of bed and I left, heading for the cafeteria. I sat down with the others and didn't say a word.

They all sat there, not talking, until finally I said, "Mary is getting dressed. She overslept."

There was a loud sigh of relief from everyone that she was okay.

When I returned home with Kosi, we settled into his new home and I started planning the fishing trip with Linda.

In the meantime I heard from my daughter Ashley that she was planning on getting married. I called her with my congratulations and hoped that I would be invited. We talked for quite a while and she informed me that David, her fiancé, and she were going to be married by a justice of the peace. David was in Marine basic training in San Diego and when he finished he was flying back to Washington. I didn't like the fact that my only daughter wasn't going to have a wedding ceremony and I could tell by Ashley's voice that she didn't either. They were short on the cash needed to have a nice wedding so I offered to give her a thousand dollars.

Ashley and her mother Cara talked about it for a couple of days, then Ashley took me up on my offer. I just asked her to let me know the prices of the reception hall, food catering and the minister.

A few days later she called me back and told me, "Mom's helping me set it up and it's going to cost a lot more."

I told Ashley that I would pay the thousand dollars. "Let's keep it within that range. Sorry but that's all I can afford right now."

Those two made all the plans and arrangements and set the date. I learned of the date from Ashley about two weeks before the wedding. I also received a call from Cara the next day.

During the conversation she said, "Ashley wants Randy to walk her down the aisle and give her away. She's afraid to tell you."

I sank into my chair and said, "What?"

Randy and Cara had been living together for about ten years and apparently Cara convinced Ashley to do this. I also found out that the wedding was going to be around $3,600 and she wanted half from me.

I called Ashley when I got off the phone with Cara and Ashley said, "I don't want to hurt your feelings but I do want Randy to give me away."

I kept my cool with her on the phone and said, "If that's what you want."

I hung up and sat there, boiling. My first thought was to not go to the wedding. I struggled with that thought until the day before the wedding. I wanted to be there but didn't know if I could sit through Randy giving my daughter away. I didn't want Ashley to be able to shove in my face that I had missed her wedding, though, so I went and acted as if it didn't bother me.

I asked Mom and Grandma to go with me to show respect. It was a struggle to convince them to go after they heard I wasn't giving Ashley away.

We went to Ashley's wedding and sat next to Cara and Randy in the front row. Randy walked her down the aisle and gave her away and I knew the approximately sixty guests there were wondering what was going on.

After Ashley and David were married the minister said, "Ashley is a lucky young lady. She has two dads. Dave, would you like the first dance with your daughter?"

Ashley and I slow danced and when the song was over it was Randy's turn. I left then, with Mom and Grandma, feeling crushed. My grandmother still to this day hasn't forgiven Ashley for that and they haven't spoken

I spoke to Ashley right after her wedding when she came over to get the money from me. I have talked to her quite a few times since then, usually to send her money. It seems as though when the money is flowing to her, we talk, and when I don't have money the communication stops. I feel I've done my best and, when Cara quits trying to make Randy Ashley's dad, Ashley will realize that. I missed two child-support payments in thirteen years, and that was when I was in the hospital. I just wish that Ashley and I could have had the opportunity to know each other without the barriers put up by Cara and Randy.

It's ironic that just a few days after the wedding Ashley called me, crying, "Randy and I are arguing and I don't know why I let him give me away."

I didn't say anything. The damage had already been done.

I had to get away from Washington for a little while, so I made quick arrangements to go fishing in California. I flew a friend from Las Vegas, Linda, there and Kosi my guide dog and I took a Greyhound bus. It was twenty-seven hours each way but it was going to be fun.

Linda and I arrived the same day and I met her at the airport. Then we went to our hotel room, which had two beds, and unpacked.

The next morning we rose early and purchased the tickets for the first boat to go out that day.

That day was a bit rough because the waves were tossing the boat around a bit. It took me all day to get my sea legs. Linda walked around as if she knew what she was doing and she made fun of me. I didn't catch anything, but Linda caught a fish.

We had our dogs tied up in the galley and checked on them now and then.

There were six guys on our boat and they claimed to be professionals. We had all put in five bucks and the person with the biggest fish would win it all. One of them caught a nice halibut early that day and went around singing, "I'm in the money; I'm in the money." He figured he had the biggest fish so it was going to be his.

Another guy had brought his wife with him, though, and with about fifteen minutes to go before we headed back, she pulled in a bigger halibut, right next to me.

I was lying on a bench in the galley on our way back and the six "professionals" were right across from me.

One of them said, "Twenty bucks apiece, buddies. We all had a personal bet and she won."

I laughed as another said, "She was just supposed to be here to wipe our brows."

A couple of them actually were very offended that she had won.

The second day I caught a nice whitefish, which turned out to be the biggest fish between Linda and me, although not on the boat.

The next morning after we had barbecued our fish and eaten them, I took off with Kosi. The bus trip again was very long and tiresome.

When I got back to Tacoma I tried to have Carmen served with divorce papers at her apartment.

When the server called me back, she said, "I have bad news. They've been evicted again and they're not here."

I tried every avenue that I knew to locate them but they had just disappeared.

CHAPTER 25

THE CHARGE IS INTERNATIONAL KIDNAPPING-HOW DO YOU PLEAD?

Now I had to wait for our trial date on October 27, 2006, to see if Nickolas was okay. Hopefully at the very least I would get weekend visitation. I was worried for Nickolas, because I knew Tim did drugs and Carmen could be influenced easily into starting them again.

I showed up for divorce court on time and Carmen wasn't there. My mother-in-law Jackie was, though, as a witness, and after being questioned by Debbie, claimed she didn't know where Nickolas or Carmen were.

We all waited for Carmen to show, thinking maybe she was stuck in traffic or looking for a parking spot. After about a half hour the judge postponed the court date until December 1. I was really worried now for Nickolas and that's all I could think about for the next month.

I had met a woman named Fran at my apartment complex and she helped me with my divorce and child custody paperwork. I didn't have the money to hire a lawyer so we used all the free resources available.

Fran and I used the County Clerks Legal Department, where I paid ten dollars an hour and we completed the parenting plan with the clerk's help.

Fran went with me to court that December day and again Carmen and Nickolas were a no-show. I was in front of the judge for around an hour pleading my case for custody of Nickolas. The judge asked me several questions as he read my proposed parenting plan.

I had proposed the traditional "every other weekend" for Carmen's visitations, and holidays were to be divided equally as well. I felt that Nickolas should be able to see his mom, and I'd give her more visitation rights when she was back on her feet. I wanted to be able to get Nickolas into a solid home environment and get him on the right path for his future.

I had moved into a house four months earlier to prepare for Nickolas to live with me. I had Fran and another woman move in as well to help persuade the judge I would be able to take care of Nickolas. I knew it would be tough to get custody of Nickolas because of my blindness. I had been warned by several professionals that usually judges are reluctant to give custody of a child to the blind parent.

The judge asked all his questions and I gave him my best answers. It seemed like an eternity while he was flipping through all the paperwork.

Fran whispered in my ear, "Don't worry. He seems like a fair judge."

He then announced in a strong, stern voice, "I'm giving you custody of Nickolas. Hope you find him quickly." I was now a divorced man.

He went on to look through the property paperwork and granted me what I had asked for – only a few items such as my dad's burial flag, my new laptop computer and other small items. I had found out that Carmen was a frequent customer of the pawn shops, and I had a feeling everything of value was already pawned.

I now had custody of Nickolas and was anxious to leave the courtroom to find him. I knew that Carmen had gotten into more trouble during that year and she was going to be hard to find.

I had no idea where Nickolas was and went directly to the Pierce County sheriff's office to have a habeas corpus warrant put out on him.

At the office we met a Deputy Sheriff, Brendan, a tall, muscular man. He listened intently to what I said about what had just happened in court. I gave him all the information I could about where I thought they could be.

After Fran and I left his office she said, "That guy is pretty big."

I pictured him kicking down a door and rescuing Nickolas from wherever he was.

I talked with Deputy Brendan every morning. As he ran out of leads we discussed other places Carmen and Nickolas might be hiding.

I was very worried about Nickolas but Deputy Brendan put me at ease, reassuring me that we'd find him soon. He never cut me off short and if he wasn't in his office he always promptly returned my phone calls.

Deputy Brendan and his office staff were trying to locate Carmen and Nickolas, but it seemed they had vanished into thin air.

One morning about two weeks later I woke up thinking, *Did she leave the country?* After all Tim was a Greek national and I figured they were still together.

I had a sick feeling in my stomach as I called the Department of US Passports in Washington, DC. I gave them Nickolas's social security number; sure enough, Carmen and Nickolas had been given passports in September. They had also paid extra to expedite the process to receive them within two weeks.

I told them Carmen had been served with child custody paperwork and she wasn't allowed to leave Washington State. They weren't sure why she had received the passports without both of Nickolas's parents signing.

I called Deputy Sheriff Brendan, told him what I had found out and asked him to check on it.

The next morning he called me and said, "I have some bad news - they both flew out of JFK Airport in September and landed in Athens, Greece, the next day."

He did go on to say that he knew where they were living and advised me to call the FBI.

I was shocked that Carmen would do this to me and, most of all, worried for Nickolas. I had heard Greece was not a very friendly country for US citizens. I immediately called the FBI. I was able to get an appointment two days later with Agent Tarna and Agent Dani.

They talked with me almost daily, telling me they knew where she was. They did a complete background check on me from head to toe because of the no-contact order. They asked me about the order and believed me when I told them how Carmen had falsely acquired it. They questioned my ex-in-laws Jackie and Farrell and found them to be uncooperative. I was told they would have gone to jail if they hadn't been so old.

Agent Tarna wrote up the arrest warrant for Carmen and Nickolas and flagged their passports. Carmen was receiving a social security check monthly for Nickolas because of my disability. One of the first things I did was to have that stopped. I figured she was living on it and maybe canceling it would flush her out of hiding.

It was a very hard Christmas that year as I waited for Nickolas to be returned to me. The Christmas tree had lots of presents under it for him, and when Christmas came and went we left the tree up. I also had Nickolas's bedroom all set up for him with new everything.

It was during this period that I woke up early one morning and heard a loud voice: "Nick is dead."

There was nobody in my room except me and I thought God was talking to me. I went out to the couch. Fran must have heard me. She came out of her bedroom and saw tears running down my face. She comforted me, telling me it must have been a nightmare. I'll never forget that morning; it was one of my worst ever.

I talked to Agent Tarna who assured me Nickolas was okay. I am thankful that Deputy Brendan, Agent Tarna and Agent Dani were there helping me keep some sort of sanity in my life.

The FBI was keeping a close watch on Carmen and Nickolas in Greece, just waiting for the arrest warrant to be signed by a federal judge for international kidnapping.

Carmen had all her money cut off except what she was getting from her mom Jackie, and she couldn't work in Greece because she didn't have a work card. It was now just a waiting game. I knew Carmen was feeling the pinch without a way to support Nickolas.

Tim and Carmen decided to fly back to the United States with Nickolas to get married. They then planned on flying back to Greece so Carmen could work. When they went to the Athens airport to fly back to the US, they were stopped by security and the three of them were taken to a private room. Security took Tim's ticket and tore it up, telling him, "Leave the airport now or go to jail."

He walked away and Carmen and Nickolas were placed on the plane. They landed in Reno, Nevada, the next day and checked into a motel room.

Tim flew into California a week later and took a Greyhound bus into Reno. The FBI had been following Carmen and Nickolas every time they had left their motel room. Carmen would call a cab and an FBI agent would be the driver without her knowledge. The FBI had learned that Carmen and Tim were planning on getting married and then flying back to Greece with Nickolas.

When Tim's bus arrived Carmen and Nickolas were waiting there. He got off the bus and the FBI took the three of them into custody just a few hours after the federal warrant was signed.

It was amazing how coordinated the FBI was, even working from different countries. I could share a lot more information on how they tracked Carmen and Tim and found them, but I'd rather not reveal their methodology.

Agent Tarna called me at home at about ten o'clock that night. She sounded very excited and said, "We have Nickolas in Reno and we'll be flying him to you on the first flight to Sea-Tac Airport."

I lay there in shock because I hadn't been informed about most of this recent activity. Then my emotions got the best of me. I was so very happy that Nickolas was now safe and coming home. I was also worried, though, about what he might have been through and hoped he was healthy. I hardly slept that night.

I received another call early the next morning. It was Agent Dani. "Nickolas is scared to death of you," she said. "We want you to place him voluntarily in foster care."

I didn't know why he was scared of me but learned later that Carmen had told him a bunch of lies about me.

I told Agent Dani, "Okay," and she said, "In these cases it usually takes a week for the kids to settle down."

Agent Dani was right on the mark with her time estimate. From the time I had Deputy Brendan, Agent Tarna, Agent Dani and all others involved behind the scenes helping me, I knew Nickolas was in good hands. The FBI didn't just fade away after bringing him back. I had tremendous support and sound advice, which I'm still getting even to this day. I still go around bragging about how professional our police and FBI agents are.

I signed the paperwork for Nickolas to go into foster care and received a call from Child Protective Services. They wanted to come over and talk.

I asked them when and she said, "Two minutes; we're around the corner."

I was in the shower so I laughed and said, "You'll have to give me five minutes so I can get dressed."

When I came out of the bathroom they were already in the living room talking to Fran. They were doing a surprise home visit, looking for anything out of the ordinary.

They walked around the house and checked out Nickolas's bedroom. They gave the house a passing grade, then we made an appointment for Nickolas and me to meet at their office in three days.

They questioned Nickolas extensively for those three days and cleared him healthwise for our supervised visitation.

When I entered the room Nickolas was already in there. I heard him say, "Hi, Dad," and my eyes started tearing up. I was able to not let the tears run down my face because of my sunglasses and I clenched my eyes shut. I was so happy to hear him and after giving him a big hug, I knew he would be okay.

I had pictures for Nickolas of his new home and his bedroom. I had also brought my dog guide Kosi with me as an icebreaker.

I left after giving Nickolas a hug and told him I'd see him in a couple days.

I learned through that visitation that he hadn't been going to school and had quite a lisp. I visited the school he was going to attend and placed him in third grade, the class he should be in.

A couple of days later I received a call from CPS saying, "Nickolas is crying and wants his daddy."

We agreed that he should have to wait until the weekend was over before coming home with me. The reasoning was that if we backed down now then he would think he could get away with anything.

I went into the CPS office the following Monday and met Nickolas in one of the supervised visitation rooms.

We chatted for a short time. Then I said, "You ready to come home now?"

He said, "I can't," and I said, "Yes, you can. It's up to you and me."

The caseworker came in quickly and told him if he wanted to go home with me he could.

Nickolas told her "yes" and she left to do the paperwork.

We grabbed his stuff and I took him to his new home.

I allowed him to take a week off of school and meet some of the kids in the neighborhood. We also had to buy him new clothes, shoes, toys and the food he liked. I soon found out that he had lived on fast foods and only ate chicken nuggets and tacos with meat and cheese. I had to introduce full-course meals at first but soon he was eating just about anything except vegetables.

I was very proud of Nickolas adjusting after the life he had had for the past year and a half to going to school and being a normal kid again. He had some problems such as his lisp but I put him in speech therapy, and after a couple of months he talked normally. It took the whole three months to catch him up to his classmates academically, but through hard work and lots of homework he did it.

One major problem he had, though, was that he was talking to the girls in his class mostly about sex. Tim had taken him to stripper bars in Greece and bought and sold drugs in front of him.

That was another problem - he knew a lot about drugs. I put him in counseling for several months and the counselor did a fantastic job of working that out of his head.

Everything was going great with Nickolas until Carmen was released pending her court date. She had a no-contact order but could call. I let them talk almost daily and pretty soon Nickolas started having problems again.

Carmen had her court date set for July, 2007 and was looking at prison time for international kidnapping. I went the day of her court hearing and it didn't look good for her.

The judge came in and sat down, then said, "I'm not happy."

Carmen slouched deeper into her chair and I noticed two FBI agents enter the courtroom. They were prepared to escort her to jail, depending on what the judge sentenced her with.

The judge prepared to sentence her after a half hour of scolding her. Then the prosecuting attorney asked the judge to let me speak.

I went in front of the judge, who was expecting me to bash Carmen, and said, "Nickolas doesn't need his mom in prison. He is doing great now and that wouldn't benefit him." The judge then changed his mind and gave her five years' probation and 120 days with an ankle bracelet.

I stood up and left, knowing that I may have just made a terrible mistake.

I told Nickolas that his mom wasn't going to jail and was going to be able to take him every other weekend for her visitation.

As soon as the visitations started, so did the trouble. It didn't take long before Nickolas started being disrespectful to me and wouldn't go to counseling.

He would say, "My mom told me I don't have to do that. I want to go live with my mom."

She had him writing down what he had for dinners and telling her who came over, and if I went to the liquor store he'd try to get the receipt and give it to her.

Carmen talked to my apartment manager and stirred up trouble with him as well. A boy about Nickolas's age lived in our apartment complex. I knew Nickolas was behind in his social skills and I started letting him start making choices on his own. I was keeping a close watch on him, but at times it was difficult with some of the decisions he was making. I let him run with the other boy and just made sure he didn't get into trouble.

It was really the first time in Nickolas' life that he wasn't attached to Carmen's hip – quite a learning experience for him. We talked almost daily about his choices and, because he has a good heart, Nickolas usually made the right decisions.

Nickolas's friend had a stepdad who was the apartment manager. It seemed odd to me that he would be out into the early hours in the parking lot where he had a broken-down RV. I was out there with Nickolas one evening and three people came up at different times for about a minute apiece. I overheard one of them ask him for a weedeater and wondered why he needed this at midnight. Then I knew what the manager was doing and I had to get Nickolas away from them.

I talked to Nickolas about drugs and watched for signs of drug use. I could tell that he wasn't using them from his actions.

I made a couple of comments to the manager, letting him know that I knew what was going on. My purpose in doing this was to make sure that he didn't have drugs around Nickolas. I also wanted him to know I was watching for signs of drug use by his stepson. As I predicted, the manager didn't like this but I didn't care what he liked.

About this time I was given four free tickets to the large waterpark nearby and wanted to take Nickolas. I didn't want to take him alone because it would be too easy to lose him because of my lack of sight. I asked the manager's girlfriend, Dawn, if she would like to take her son and at the same time keep an eye on Nickolas. She wasn't bad looking and I was told she would look pretty good in a bikini. I thought, *Why not? This could give her boyfriend more time to sell his drugs.*

On the third of July, 2008 I took Dawn and her son along with Nickolas to the waterpark. It was very clear to me that they seldom did anything away from the apartments.

When the boys weren't looking, we flirted as if we were on our first date. I listened to her talk about the drug problems her boyfriend had and the physical abuse she and her son were taking from him. I felt sympathy for her but I wasn't going to get involved other than to offer her advice to leave him.

When we returned home late that night she went to her apartment and I went to mine.

About half an hour later there was a knock on my door. She was standing there with her son and she said, "He kicked us out. Can we stay here for tonight?"

I didn't really have a choice, so I let them in.

The next morning when he found that she had stayed with me I started getting harassed. I knew it was time to move when his actions became more erratic. One moment he would be fine. Other times he was high on drugs and unpredictable.

I was served two times with sexual harassment charges from Dawn and each time she didn't appear for court. She let me know that it wasn't her choice to file these and was sorry. She went on to say that she had to do this so she and her son had a place to live. The night we spent together she and her son mentioned that they would like to move in with me and Nickolas, but I told her "no."

She called me once telling me what a great time she had had that night and that she wished things were different.

He made sure that we didn't talk to or see each other and continued his own harassment on me. I eventually called the owner and told him my side of the story. The owner came over the next evening and we talked in person. He didn't believe me that Dawn had been kicked out and had spent the night and he asked me to move. I told him I would be out the following month.

I started looking for another apartment and filled out a couple of applications. I looked for apartments that had nice cars parked outside and a family-oriented atmosphere.

In the meantime I was constantly getting harassed by the manager and he was starting to take it out on Nickolas.

Carmen and I hardly had any civil communication and she was able to turn Nickolas against me.

Almost daily after talking to his mom on the phone I heard him say, "I want to go live with my mom."

It got to the point where I was fighting a losing battle with Nickolas. I sat him down during one of his tantrums and told him, "I'll let you go live with your mom for two weeks. If you want to live with her after that it's your choice."

I made it perfectly clear that I wanted him to live with me but left him to make his decision.

Two weeks later I called him and asked him if he had decided.

Nickolas said, "I want to live with Mom."

I already knew the answer because Carmen, Jackie and Farrell were buying him anything and everything he wanted. I wasn't going to go this route with Nickolas and told him "okay."

I went to court a couple of weeks later and handed over physical custody of Nickolas to Carmen. I had had custody of him for almost two years and turned him into a normal kid again. Nickolas was now academically level with his peers and liked school. I had also put him on a few sports teams and stopped him from talking about sex to girls. I did all I could do for him and I'm hoping it sticks with him throughout life.

Carmen and Nickolas came over to the apartment and I gave them everything that Nickolas wanted to take with him. I didn't keep anything except a couple of pictures of him playing sports. I then gave away most of my possessions to the residents of the apartment complex. I was washing my hands of Tacoma and heading for Oregon to make a fresh start.

I lived in Oregon for only a few months but it didn't work out. I still worried about Nickolas and wanted to be closer to him. I moved back to Tacoma and rented a duplex about ten miles from him.

At this time Kosi didn't want to guide me anymore so I retired him, giving him to the owner of the duplex so I could see him once in a while.

What else could happen to me? I wondered. Even my dog guide didn't want to live with me.

I lived there for a few months and I knew right away it was a bad move. Carmen had a couple of boyfriends now, and it was clear she didn't want me around Nickolas. She wanted him to have a new daddy and she wanted to hurt me as much as possible.

Nickolas was embarrassed about my blindness and didn't want his friends to see me. He also hated taking the bus and, because I didn't drive, that's how we traveled.

I could tell that Carmen was taking some type of stimulant and was paranoid about me finding out. I had a choice of sticking around or moving away from Nickolas and letting him go on with his life. I hope that Jackie keeps a better eye on her daughter Carmen and Nickolas until he decides to see me again. It was very clear to me that they preferred I move out of their area, so I started making plans to move.

Leaving Nickolas was a very hard decision. I feel that I let down a lot of people who had helped us. Nickolas was so brainwashed by now that he rarely even talked to me on the telephone.

I called up my friend Fran and asked if she and her roommate could put me up for a week or so in Florida. I was hoping that was far enough away from Carmen and her harassment.

CHAPTER 26

IS SUNNY FLORIDA FAR ENOUGH AWAY?

I landed in Fort Myers, Florida, on March 5, 2009, with my three suitcases. My Florida friends Fran and Nancy met me at the baggage claim area and I must have looked like a wreck. I went outside immediately to have a cigarette and took my Bengals cap off.

Fran said, "Put that cap back on. Your hair is a mess."

I put it back on and I heard Nancy say, "Jeez, Fran. He's been on a plane all day. What do you expect?"

I was wearing jeans and a long sleeved shirt expecting the temperature to be in the eighties, but it was ninety-five degrees and I was starting to sweat. We took off for the town of Nokomis and, when we were halfway there and stopped for a bite to eat, I changed into shorts and a short-sleeved shirt.

I ordered my bacon double cheeseburger and noticed Fran and Nancy ordered salads with no meat. When I questioned them Fran said, "We're mostly vegetarians and hardly ever eat meat."

I just shrugged it off as "you don't know what you're missing" and continued to eat my bacon cheeseburger.

When we drove up to Nokomis, they guided me to my room and showed me the couch I was going to sleep on until I found my own place. The Florida room was comfortable, with a TV, and I settled in for the night.

The next morning Fran and I went shopping for food that I would eat, mostly meat products. Then we went to Kmart and I bought a pair of flip-flops.

For the next two weeks Fran and Nancy made me feel pretty comfortable, but I needed to get my own place. Fran and I went to the Venice/Nokomis Eagles Club a couple of times a week but, because of the cigarette smoke, she didn't like going. I started losing weight because I felt strange asking them to cook me something different for dinners and mostly ate what they were eating: bean sprout salads, rice and low-fat everything.

I asked Fran to drive me around and help me find a place.

After two weeks I finally found a little one-bedroom apartment that was connected to a house where an elderly woman and her disabled son lived. It was furnished and was perfect for a single guy.

I moved in the next week and started thinking about finding a job, making friends and having a social life. I called the local cab company and filled up my food and liquor cabinets. I pretty much stayed drunk for the next week and ate a whole lot of spaghetti and meatballs. I'd usually cook scrambled eggs with bacon in the morning, and for lunch I'd cook up something and make a drink. I had my computer hooked up and went on line looking for dates with the local women.

I did go up to the Eagles once by myself by cab and tried to meet people that way. I was sitting there when a woman sat down with me. I had talked to her before and knew she was married. She got up now and then and on her way back to sit down would come up behind me and rub her breasts up against my back. She'd run her hand up and down my leg and kiss me on the neck. Because she was married I didn't want anything to do with her, so I called a cab and went home.

I found out the next day that her husband was there observing her flirting and was just about ready to step in and stop it. That was the last time I went back there, and now I really didn't have any place to hang out anymore. Everywhere else was too far away for me to pay a cab and the women were hard to strike up a conversation with because I was blind. I didn't have my dog guide anymore so there was no longer my favorite icebreaker. When you're by yourself it's not easy going to a lounge and meeting people. They don't seem to approach you and I sure wasn't going to go from table to table and ask, "Any ladies want to chat?"

I was able to find a couple of women online who I dated, but they were into more than I wanted in meeting people. One took me to a party that was outdoors, and when I got there I had to undress because it was a nudist camp!

I did have a good time chatting with one of the women at the camp and learned a lot about their lifestyle. I felt pretty comfortable in the nude because everyone else was naked, too. There are strict rules at these parties and nobody touches without the other person's consent. It's not a free-for-all for sex, but more like a social party without the clothes. Of course some people go off and do their own thing, but it's discreet and very natural. I wasn't ashamed of my body so I didn't feel I had anything to hide. The next day, though, I sure did wish that I had put on some bug spray. I had bug bites everywhere you can imagine. I had gone to a nudist beach in Oregon a few times but the bugs were never that bad.

I really wanted to settle down with a nice woman, and I started getting depressed living alone.

One evening I was cooking up a tuna casserole and accidentally missed the colander and poured half of the noodles in the sink. I didn't have food to waste and I just lost it. I went to my couch and started crying. I was talking to God and telling him I couldn't take this any longer, being blind. I knew I had done it to myself but I was getting tired of being alone, no extra cash and blind. I wanted to go to work, but when you're blind hardly anyone will give you a chance to prove yourself.

One day, while I was doing some food shopping, I met a nice woman named Lisa at the store. She stopped to talk to me while I was waiting for my bus and we kind of hit it off. I got her phone number and we chatted a couple of times before we went out.

It took a while to get together because we both were broke. She was a teacher and we all know how little they make. She knew my birthday was coming up and I was going to be alone for it, so she saved a bit of cash and we had a nice evening with dinner and a couple of drinks. We danced a little, then she drove me home. She kissed me on the cheek and told me goodnight. We remained good friends until I moved a couple of months later.

I was feeling pretty good about myself with meeting friends without the pressure of sex, and my drinking had almost stopped. However I was running out of money because I wasn't working yet, and I found it harder and harder to buy food. I had to start going to foodbanks to survive and was losing weight – about five pounds a month.

I went to the Venice Senior Friendship Center and talked to Ola, the social worker there. Ola was a great help and found me a volunteer named Patti.

Patti called me the next day and offered her services to me. I needed help reading my mail, writing checks for my bills and going shopping, as well as just some interaction with people.

Patti became my best friend and she helped me in every way that she could. She got me out of the house that I literally was wasting my life away in. We went to a drum circle on Venice Beach a couple of times which was very cool. The organizers would draw a big circle in the sand and drummers from all over came and joined in with all kinds of different drums. The public – most times in the hundreds – brought their lawn chairs with their coolers and had a good time. There would be hula hoopers, belly dancers and people in costumes in the circle as well. It was a fun atmosphere, like a carnival, and it was free.

I usually could keep Patti out of my kitchen cabinets when they were empty. She tried to find out if I had food, but unless I had just gone shopping or come from the foodbank, I wouldn't let her look. When I did have food, I lined up the corn in one row, beans in another, and so on down the line. I never had too much to have to worry about but it impressed Patti tremendously when I could find a can of corn. If a blind person doesn't keep really organized then, when he grabs a can of something, most of the time it is something else. Once I was making a tuna casserole and instead of grabbing the cream of mushroom soup it turned out to be tomato soup. I didn't have food to waste so I just used the tomato soup and ate it. It was awful, but when that's all you have, you eat it.

We also went to lunch, shopping and just had good conversations.

One day Patti checked out my cabinets while I was outside having a cigarette.

She came out pretty upset and said, "You have no food."

Her voice was trembling a bit and I could tell she was really bothered. She grabbed her purse and left. About an hour later she came back with bags of groceries for me. Patti helped me survive at this time by buying me food, and I wouldn't have eaten without her help.

Patti is a dear friend to this day and she will always have a warm place in my heart.

Patti encouraged me to apply for another dog guide, so I called Southeastern Guide Dogs in Palmetto, Florida. I spoke with Rita who mailed me the application which Patti helped fill out.

On weekdays Southeastern has "puppy petting" to help the puppies get socialized with people. People go there and just pet puppies and walk them around the campus. Patti wanted to pet the puppies, so we packed a lunch and went. I met Rita in person while we were there.

Rita signed me up for the next class, starting in September, with the class lasting twenty-eight days.

Southeastern Guide Dogs is totally funded by donations, so the students receiving dog guides don't pay a penny. They house all the students for twenty-eight days, feed them three square meals a day, and have approximately one trainer per three students.

I walked into Southeastern Guide Dogs on September 3, 2009, with Patti and my two suitcases.

We went into the students' lounge area and I heard, "Hello. What's your name?"

At first she sounded like a little girl, but then I realized it came from a woman with a heavy southern accent.

I said, "Dave, and what's yours?"

She replied, "Holly. I'm a student."

I excused myself and went to the room I was staying in for the next twenty-eight days. After Patti helped me unpack my clothes, she left and I went out into the student lounge to find out more about this other student with the pretty voice. Most of the seven students were there chatting. We learned that our class would have five women and four men. Two students were arriving a week later as they needed less training. We were given our orientation around the campus and a brief description of our daily training. It was an exciting day as everyone prepared to receive their new dog guides the next day.

I was able to find the smokers' area and found out I was the only cigarette smoker in the class. One of the male students smoked a pipe, so I met him out there and found out he was from the Carolinas.

It wasn't long before Holly walked out to visit with us at the smokers' table. She was quite the friendly person, and from her voice I could tell she was always wearing a smile. She and I introduced ourselves formally and I found out that she was widowed and close to my age.

I had grown tired of the single life and decided that if I met a nice woman who was single I'd give it a chance. Holly asked if I was single and from that moment on we hit it off.

Holly has some vision so she was able to check me out, but I wanted to find out what she looked like, so after I finished my cigarette I asked her to guide me back into the student lounge. She stood up and let me take her arm. We went to the door and I "accidentally" bumped into her backside. By doing that I found out she stood around five feet four, had a nice body and shoulder-length hair. It's amazing how much you can find out about someone just by "accidentally" bumping into them.

Holly was just my type and apparently she was attracted to me, too. We started hanging around together every spare minute we could. We went through the ritual of finding out what each other's interests were in a relationship; we were both looking for the same things in life.

Monday came pretty quickly and we all received our dog guides. I was given Bingo, a vizsla, and Holly received an almost pure white Labrador retriever named Oreo. The other students received Labradors and Australian shepherd guides. We bonded with our dog guides for an hour or so in our rooms and then it was time to go to work.

Southeastern Guide Dogs had us on a pretty rigorous schedule of training. We woke at six in the morning and walked our dog guides. Then it was time to clean up a bit and prepare for a seven o'clock breakfast.

The breakfasts were always good and consisted mainly of bacon, eggs, hash browns, cold or hot cereal and fruit juice. We also had the option of coffee or milk and there was always plenty of food to fill your belly.

After breakfast we fed our dog guides and usually had about half an hour to finish getting ready for the day of training or go watch some television. Usually Holly and I met in the student lounge and talked. Generally, I got there first and Holly came a few minutes later.

She always sat next to me and I'd say, "Marking your territory?"

We'd laugh and let the dogs play.

Then we all got onto a bus and had a different daily location to go train. There were usually three trainers and we took turns on routes.

Different students alternated with the various trainers: Leanne, Karen (Holly called her "Sarge"), Jennifer, Kate and Marissa – they were all professional and I could tell right away they knew what they were doing.

I was primarily assigned to Leanne, Karen and Marissa.

Karen was a great trainer with a heart of gold. She was able to build my confidence and always showed all the students respect. If a mistake was made or you were confused on your direction, she could settle you down and correct you without making you feel it was all your fault.

Leanne was also a good trainer and a new apprentice. I found it amusing at times that she was so obsessed with our safety. I used to give her a hard time in jest but she couldn't get used to my joking personality. I could tell she loved her job and she would do anything for her students.

I think she learned as much from me as I learned from her.

Marissa was a good trainer as well and it was obvious she really enjoyed her job. I don't know how she knew it, but if I was feeling down she could always tell and perk me up with a laugh or two.

At first we traveled the campus, then eventually we were all traveling through malls, neighborhoods and busy city areas. Then after morning training we settled down at a restaurant or headed back to the campus for lunch.

One of the days when we were traveling through the mall, my dog guide Bingo was distracted by a female mannequin. Bingo took me right up to the mannequin and stopped. Jennifer was my trainer that day and she didn't say a word. I reached forward to find out if I was at the wall where I was supposed to take a right turn. Then I heard Jennifer start to laugh as she saw the look on my face as I touched the mannequin. Apparently I was feeling up the mannequin; I couldn't figure out what it was. Jennifer knew I had experience with dog guides and, like Karen, would let me make mistakes and work my way out of them.

In the afternoon we walked our dog guides and then headed out for more training. We returned around four or so and fed our dogs. Then we ate dinner and had the rest of the evening to relax.

Holly and I became almost inseparable during our training and spare time. One day after training she tiptoed into my room and gave me a very nice hug.

She whispered in my ear, "I love you."

I was a bit shocked at first because I hadn't heard that from a woman in many years.

I said, "I love you, too."

We kissed and she left my room before she got caught. We weren't allowed in the other students' rooms, because

Southeastern Guide Dogs wanted to keep the hanky panky to a minimum. This is the policy of most other dog guide schools as well.

"This is not a hotel but a training center for independence," I heard from one of the other schools I attended. There was a good chance if you were caught performing "adult activities" you could be sent home without your dog guide. Holly and I didn't want to take that chance.

We went on our first date on a weekend off from training and spent the day at a mall walking around. Our next date, which we set up for the following weekend, was at a hotel lounge. We ended up getting a room and "relaxing" for a few hours before having to go back to school that evening.

The school staff was fully aware that we had become more than just friends and made it a point to keep us together on the bus, on training routes and meals. One evening Leanne, before leaving, let us know there were cameras just about everywhere around the school.

"Be careful," she told us.

On the third Sunday Holly invited her friend Joy and her stepdaughter, Melissa, to the campus to meet me. They drove down separately because Melissa had two sons and there wasn't room for all of us in one car.

The first time I met Joy she was a bit skeptical of Holly and me being together. Joy thought that we were just going to go our separate ways after the training had ended.

Melissa, however, had no intention of letting Holly and me ever build a relationship. I soon found out that after Holly's husband passed away five months earlier, Melissa and her husband, Darell, moved to Brooksville. I also learned that Darell wasn't working and Holly was paying a large portion of their bills. Holly was their meal ticket.

At the restaurant Melissa asked me what plans I had with Holly.

I told her, "Well, we're probably going to be married within two weeks."

I was just joking but Melissa took great offense to this and proclaimed, "The hell you are!"

I had already been warned about Melissa and just laughed it off. This made her even madder and I knew she was going to be trouble.

We had a nice dinner after that and Joy drove Holly, Bingo, Oreo and me back to Southeastern.

It wasn't long after that dinner that Holly and I began to plan future trips after the training was over. I lived in Nokomis about 100 miles south of where she lived. I was also starting my new job as soon as I graduated with my dog guide. When we realized how hard it would be to commute back and forth, we decided one of us would be moving in with the other. Since I had few ties in Nokomis, I would be moving north with Holly to Brooksville.

We all graduated except for one student. She just couldn't get the training down correctly and had to leave without her dog guide.

My friend Patti was there for my graduation and afterwards drove Bingo and me home.

Joy and Holly arrived at my place the next morning. We packed up all of my belongings and headed for Brooksville.

CHAPTER 27

FINALLY AT PEACE
WITH MYSELF

When we arrived in Brooksville we went directly to Holly's home in Cloverleaf Farms, a small community near the west coast of Florida. Holly showed me around inside her home and it was quite nice, with three bedrooms, two baths and a screened porch to keep the bugs away while enjoying the warm days and nights. We put most of my belongings away and settled in for the evening.

The next morning Holly drove me around the park in her golf cart. I wasn't sure at first about getting into the golf cart with her because of her low vision (she can see better sometimes than others, but not well enough to keep her driver's license), but she did fine. We only went about ten miles an hour.

I was introduced to some of Holly's friends who were outside driving around or doing yardwork in the park. I've never lived in a gated community and noticed most of the people had golf carts. It is really a nice way of going to the clubhouses, visiting friends within the park, and traveling to the lakes to fish or relax. It is also much safer than walking on the side of the roads; a few of the senior citizens have less than 20/20 vision. It cuts down on accidents, too, because a couple of the people in the park don't exactly stay in their lanes. I'm not crazy about getting mowed down from behind when walking on the side of the road. Walking is not part of my passtime here; I like the protection of being inside a golf cart.

Holly and I have been in a couple of spontaneous golf cart races, which are the high point of the day for some of the park residents. They take it so personally around here that if they lose, sometimes they'll avoid you for days.

Golf carts are like a status symbol here in Cloverleaf, and some people have them tricked-out like Peter-bilt semi-trucks, in Harley Davidson colors, like BMWs and so on. It is mostly safe; if we crashed there would be minimal damage because top speeds are around twenty miles per hour. Holly has her cart tricked-out with chrome push bumpers, larger-than-normal tires and a rollover bar. One man in the park even wears black racing gloves whenever he drives his golf cart.

Our first month living together was very nice. The only problem we had was with Melissa trying to break us up.

I had been single for so long it took some adjusting on my part to having a female around all the time.

I wasn't able to take the job I had been offered because of transportation, so I started my own business to keep busy. I have an on-line store that provides independent living products for the blind/low vision and senior citizens: magnifiers, talking products, kitchen aids and everyday household items. It keeps me occupied and at the same time I'm rewarded by helping people save a little money.

The majority of people in Brooksville are retired and there isn't much of a night life. I found it hard at first hanging around Holly's friends, who seemed to all have at least ten years on me. Holly had established a comfort zone among her friends and I wasn't used to such a sedate life.

One of my favorite couples in Cloverleaf is Roy and Jeanne. Since transportation is such a hassle here, Roy and Jeanne sometimes offer to take us to places in a pinch.

Roy is a great guy who has lived in Brooksville for over sixty years now, and I've learned a lot about the history of the town from him. I have always liked discovering the history of places and I enjoy listening to Roy.

His girlfriend Jeanne is a nice woman who truly loves Roy, and she would drop everything to give us a hand. We can always count on her to take my packages to the post office, fix up some really tasty crab legs, or grab me a burger when Holly and she are out shopping.

Every Wednesday Roy and Jeanne are prompt at picking us up for the Wednesday-night dinner at one of our local churches. At first I found it hard to go to the dinners at a church I wasn't attending, but once I met some of the people it became relaxing to socialize with them.

I went to Holly's church dinners, potlucks and dances at the clubhouses, and family barbecues, but after a while I became less enthusiastic about going. It seemed as if I was hearing the same old gossip time and time again. I don't fault anyone for it as there is only so much to talk about in this small town.

We sat down one evening and discussed finding couples our own age who were a bit livelier. Holly agreed with me; now our only problem was getting out to enjoy a nightlife. The bus system (Trans/Hernando) shuts down at three-thirty in the afternoon in Brooksville and the alternative was a taxi. The cost of a taxi is eight dollars just to open the door and if you want to go to a couple of places it will cost a small fortune.

I wasn't quite used to having little or no transportation. In Washington State they provide excellent services for their disabled and senior citizens. The Pierce County Shuttle in Tacoma provided rides from five in the morning until midnight, seven days a week, 365 days a year for only 75 cents.

Here in Brooksville transportation is provided from seven in the morning until three-thirty in the afternoon, excluding weekends and holidays. This makes it difficult to schedule appointments with doctors because, if your appointment runs over, you're left finding your own way home.

I also have one of the Trans/Hernando drivers mad at me for some reason (I still can't figure it out) and he is almost always slow at picking me up. Then he takes the long route to get me home. It could be that one ride many months ago his wife Jackie, a driver as well for Trans/Hernando, picked me up after I got my hair cut. When I entered the bus she asked me the address of where we were. I wasn't sure and told her so. I figured that she must know it as she had picked me up. She became very sarcastic with me, insisting I give her the address.

This took me out of my good mood and I told her to look at her paperwork. It wasn't long before we were arguing back and forth and I started finding it amusing. That made her even more argumentative and I just ignored her.

Holly and I would cross our fingers with each ride we set up that one of these two drivers would not have us on their schedule to pick us up. We knew if they were to pick us up, our day would be spent waiting for them to get us. The other drivers, one in particular, Eddie, always were cheerful and professional.

In January we received a letter in the mail from Trans/Hernando Transit that Hernando County Transit would be taking over transit services. Holly and I read the letter and assumed that service hours were going to be cut as that was the talk of the Hernando County Commissioners for the last year.

We waited for March and called to schedule our first ride with this new company.

I called to schedule a ride for the next day and Beverly answered the phone from Hernando County Transit.

When I spoke with Beverly I was pleasantly surprised that she was not insulting and was very informative. I learned during that phone conversation that Hernando County Transit is going to provide its riders with additional hours during the week and is hopeful to add Saturday service. It was also nice to have them listen to me, as some people think blind people don't know what they are talking about.

Now I'm not a stupid person, and neither are the majority of blind people, but for some reason some people think because we're blind, we're also "deaf and dumb." Here's an example: I can't even count the number of times I'll be waiting for a bus and someone will shout from about a foot away, "What bus are you waiting for?"

I don't take this personally – I figure they are just trying to help – but it just about knocks me out of my shoes.

I usually just smile and say, "Shh, I can hear just fine."

Twice, though, in the past few years my fist connected with someone's face as an automatic reflex. Fortunately both times they were men (whose voices are much louder than most women's.) The second time I hit the man so hard it knocked him to the ground and I had to help him up. All I could do was apologize and make sure he was okay. I hate waiting for a bus and not being able to get in my car and drive.

Transportation is my hardest adjustment to blindness. Before I lost my sight when I wanted to go anywhere I'd just grab my keys and go. Now I have to plan at least one day in advance, which makes it tough if you're craving a cheeseburger.

My way of stress reduction before my blindness was to go to the ocean, fish, or just drive around with the radio playing. Now that isn't an option. I have to ask others for assistance. I feel as if I'm bothering people when I ask for a ride. Most of the time they let me know they're not happy about getting their butts off the couch. In some cases if I have to go badly enough, twenty dollars or more will get me a ride, but only after I hear a story about how much I'm interrupting their TV show.

I've learned to schedule my time and get everything done in a couple of hours or just go without.

Holly asks Joy to take her to the store if she needs to go as well. Most people who do take us somewhere such as a restaurant insist on sitting there with us and getting a free meal. I notice that these people always order the most expensive item on the menu, and one woman orders enough so that she can take food home. This is so she won't have to cook for her husband. We use her as the last resort, but sometimes she is our only option. We usually hire a driver to take us out on a weekend night and he comes and gets us at a specified time.

I could hear Holly coming to life when we were out listening to music, dancing and socializing with people our age. We started going out monthly and having a good time meeting new friends and just plain getting away from Cloverleaf. Our relationship really started blossoming at that time. She was happier and so was I.

Holly usually goes out shopping during the day as I work my business, so we have time apart and she can see her friends. However the night is now ours to share.

My new business is starting to pick up and now is keeping me occupied. I wanted to do something for Holly and let everyone see how much I loved her. I decided to have a dinner/dance at one of Cloverleaf's clubhouses right before Christmas, 2009. In the meantime, Holly's step-daughter Melissa, and Darrell, Melissa's husband, were really trying my patience. They would come over unannounced with their twin four-year-old boys and take over the house.

According to Holly, "In the South we open our house as if it is theirs. It's Southern hospitality."

I put up with this for a couple months, but when I crawled into bed one evening and there were potato chips between the sheets left by the boys, that crossed my line of tolerance. The jumping on the furniture, spilling food and fruit juice, and breaking stuff as they ran through the house unsupervised was too much for me.

I got that under control really quickly, but I became the arch enemy of Melissa and Darrell. I didn't care because they had already irritated my last nerve.

It was about this time that my daughter Ashley and I started talking again. She and her husband were having marital problems and they had split up. Ashley needed a few hundred dollars every month to supplement her loss of income. I sent her money monthly and everything was going well between us. We talked almost weekly and she started calling me "Dad" again.

I was communicating with Nickolas, too, and he was doing fine.

Life was really good, I loved my Holly, both of my kids were talking to me, and business was picking up.

We were selling tickets to our dinner/dance and had picked out a live band in Brooksville that I had heard a month before. We chose the music that we wanted played, mostly sixties and seventies.

We advertised with flyers at local establishments and hired a chef to cook the meals. We also had eight friends volunteer to decorate and assist with helping serve and make sure our guests were comfortable.

The night before our dinner/dance, Holly and I were cuddled up on the couch watching TV when the phone rang.

I was comfortable lying there and said, "Just let it ring," but Holly decided to answer it.

The caller was my ex-wife Carmen.

Holly put it on speaker phone and I heard Carmen screaming at Holly to give me the phone. I was thinking, "Damn, Carmen, only you could screw up a perfect evening."

I took the receiver and listened while Carmen screamed at me for a minute or so.

Then I just said, "Let me talk to Nickolas."

She gave the phone to Nickolas and when he cussed me out I hung up on him.

I'm still not sure what it was about. All I can figure is that Carmen had turned him against me again. I don't understand why some women do this. It hurts everyone involved, especially the children. However, I shrugged it off for that night and just focused on our dinner/dance the next day.

We had sold enough tickets in the park through the newspaper and TV ads that we were going to break even. It wasn't about the money, it was about Holly and me showing the world we were a couple in love.

The next morning Holly was a wreck, trying to finish up all the little details herself. Half of our help didn't show up on time to set up the clubhouse and that made Holly even more anxious. I tried to keep her calm and just have a good time with it, but she was frantic. We had to help with the decorating with our friends, which put us way behind. When we had about one hour before the dinner was supposed to start, Joy took over and let Holly and me come home to get ready. Holly was still a nervous wreck wondering if everything was going to be set up perfectly, if the cook was going to show, and if everyone who had bought tickets was going to turn up. She wanted a full house and the food to be great.

We finally left our home five minutes before the start of our event and headed up to the clubhouse in our golf cart. We were very fortunate to leave with five minutes remaining, because Holly kept changing her clothes and couldn't decide which shoes matched her outfit.

When we arrived the place was full of people and everyone was socializing. Holly looked around - the place looked beautiful.

I just smiled and said, "See? No worries. It's going to be a nice evening."

Holly and I went around introducing ourselves, and I couldn't help hearing people say how beautiful she looked. I got a few compliments on my clothes as well. I give all the credit to Holly because she had picked them out for me. I wasn't even sure what colors I was wearing. I just trusted her judgement.

We mingled for a short time, then I grabbed Holly's hand and headed for the stage. We walked hand in hand and I introduced Holly and myself.

I gave the itinerary of the events for the evening then said, "Is everyone hungry?"

The crowd of about sixty all shouted, "Yes!"

And I said, "After the band gets their food, let's eat."

The dinner went very well and people raved about how tasty it was. The meal consisted of spaghetti and meatballs, veggies, homemade garlic bread and a nice fresh salad. We had soft music playing in the background, and after about an hour everyone was ready to dance.

I handed the microphone to Vic, the main singer, and he took over welcoming everyone. The band was made up of three singers, with Vic being the main voice and two women, Mandy and Tallie, singing backup as well as solos. There was also a six-piece band that didn't miss a note all evening long.

Vic and the band did a great job livening everyone up, and soon most of the people were dancing.

Mandy and Tallie, both attractive women, had the full attention of the men in the audience and changed costumes a couple of times for certain songs.

Tallie was singing a solo and she went out into the crowd and sang a romantic song to a man in his early seventies who was sitting next to me. He was getting turned on by Tallie and all everyone could do was laugh at his facial expressions.

After Tallie finished the song he leaned over to me and said, "I think she likes me. I'm going to ask her out on a date."

I tried to explain to him that it was part of the show and she was already married. I also told him that she was thirty something and could be his grandchild. He didn't want to hear any of that and insisted that she liked him. For days after the dance he asked Holly and me for her phone number, but we wouldn't give it to him.

After the first intermission the band started playing music again. I had asked Vic to play a slow dance for Holly and me.

He called for us to come up and announced, "This song is for you two."

Holly wasn't aware that I had requested this and, being a little shy, she hesitated at first. I took her by her hand and pulled her close to me under the lights. The whole place stopped as we slow-danced, and when I kissed her everyone applauded.

It was very romantic and I proclaimed my love for Holly. She had tears running down her face and when the song was over she whispered in my ear, "I love you so much."

We danced and mingled with our guests for the rest of the evening. After our dance ended we cleaned up and went home, knowing everyone had a great time.

It was very exhausting throwing the dinner/dance and it took a couple of days of relaxing around the house to recoup.

The next weekend we were asked to walk in the Brooksville Christmas parade with our guide dogs. Bingo and Oreo were dressed up as reindeer. It was a lot of fun listening to all the kids saying, "Look, Mom, here come the reindeers".

A couple of days later Holly sat down with me and asked, "What are we doing for Christmas?"

I hadn't really thought about it a lot, as it was still fifteen days off. She said that we had a couple of invitations - one to her friend Kathy's place and the other to Melissa and Darrell's home.

Melissa and I had had a falling out earlier that month and I strongly objected to going there. However, after a couple of days of Holly asking me, I finally gave in.

Holly and I made all the homemade candy, turkey, dressing and several dishes and went to the dinner on Christmas Eve.

There were about ten of us there and we let the bad blood subside for the evening. We enjoyed opening the gifts and sat down for dinner. I had just finished one plate and was waiting for it to settle before going for seconds. The phone rang and Melissa answered it.

The call was from Melissa's biological mother and after Melissa hung up she told Holly and me that we had to leave. We were asked to leave the food and come back the next evening as there was tons of food left. We agreed, expecting to return. That didn't happen, though, because Melissa's mother stayed there for a couple days and enjoyed our food.

That was the last straw for me. Melissa and Darrell moved to Fort Myers a short time later when Melissa was offered a better job.

It was about this time as well that I wasn't able to send Ashley money. I tried to explain to her that it was only for one month, but the phone calls stopped from Ashley when the money stopped.

During the winter and into early spring Holly could tell I was concerned about Nickolas. I just wanted to see him and make sure he was healthy. I also didn't want him to think that I had abandoned him.

Holly and I flew to Washington in May 2010 to visit Nickolas and I introduce her to my family. I called Nickolas several times while we were there, but he didn't return my phone calls.

Although we didn't see Nickolas, we had a great time in Washington for those three days. I introduced Holly to my grandmother, Mom and stepfather Fritz. The rest of my relatives couldn't find the time. It didn't exactly shock me as our extended family has argued for many years. Grandma used to be able to keep the family together for holidays and special events, but now it's out of her control. We had a great time otherwise. We took my grandmother and Uncle Johnny to dinner and spent a lot of time catching up on family matters with them.

The Pacific Northwest is a beautiful place and Holly was able to see another part of the country instead of just Florida. On one of her "good eye" days she saw Mt. Rainier, with its snow-capped summit towering above the mountain ranges. I also took her to a few of the historical sites in Tacoma and, of course, she went shopping.

Holly must have told me twenty times how beautiful the landscape and colors were in Washington. I also felt good when she mentioned how friendly the people were. When we left I was glad I had showed her where I had grown up and had spent my life prior to meeting her.

Life is going great for Holly and me, with hardly any interference from our friends and family. We have settled down and life is becoming very comfortable.

Holly had convinced me to go to church with her one Sunday. A friend of ours, Beverly, invited us to her church and we accepted the invitation.

When we arrived on July 4, 2010 at the Brooksville First Presbyterian Church, which is often called "the friendliest church in Brooksville," we were met with open arms. Pastor Andrew Beery and his wife, Lori, immediately made me feel at ease. We met quite a few members of the congregation at the potluck immediately following the services.

Holly and I were given a ride back home and I made the decision to continue attending on Sundays. In September 2010 I became a member of the church and for the first time in my life I was baptized.

Holly and I have donated many bags of groceries to our church to help feed the needy. It makes me feel really good to finally be able to give back to the church for all the food I received from *them* when *I* needed it.

As for Nickolas I have finally thrown my arms up in the air hoping that in a few years when he matures he'll come looking for me. I just can't handle it any longer – the disrespect from him. I will let Jackie and Carmen raise him to the best of their abilities. I just hope that he stays out of trouble and takes the path I was leading him down while I had custody.

I haven't talked to Ashley in almost a year and don't know much of what she is doing.

Mom did call me a few months ago and said, "Hi, Grandpa."

I wasn't sure why she said that but after the silence she said, "You do know Ashley is pregnant?"

I said, "No. I haven't talked to her."

She said she read it on Facebook and Ashley was due in December. Through the grapevine I heard that she was having a baby girl, but after a few attempts at calling her we still haven't spoken.

My sisters Barbara, Connie and I now talk to each other regularly and the three of us met at Connie's place in South Carolina for Thanksgiving. It was the first time we had spent the holidays together since we were teenagers.

Barbara and her husband, Connie and her friend Kelly, Holly and I, and Connie's daughter Christiana, along with her friend who was also there, had a great time visiting and seeing each other again.

Mom and I had a good relationship and I called her weekly. We all three wished Mom and Fritz could have joined us for Thanksgiving but it didn't happen. We did call up to Washington and talked to Grandma, Mom, Fritz, my Uncle Johnny and my half-brother Steven and wished them a happy Thanksgiving as well. They all met at Mom and Fritz's home to enjoy the holiday.

Steven now lives in Seattle and we kept in contact monthly. He is successful, working for a cruise company and travels frequently. Whenever he goes on a cruise I tell him to watch "Titanic" the night before and we laughed.

My half-brother Loyd and I don't talk that often, probably because of the age difference and he now resides in North Dakota.

We made plans for the whole family to meet in one place next year for Thanksgiving, and I hope it will happen. We're all spread out throughout the US, and hopefully we can meet at Barbara's next year.

For Christmas we traveled south 200 miles and spent time with Melissa, Darrell and the twins. Holly and I had a great three days visiting them and all the past problems have been forgiven.

Holly and I are now engaged and we're very supportive of each other. I also like waking up each morning to us sharing, "I love you" and Holly asking me what I want for breakfast. She is a great cook and I've added a few pounds since living here.

I have learned through my pastor how to forgive and forget and let my anger go. I now let life happen as it happens and don't sweat the small stuff. As I sit here finally at peace with myself at 3 AM, with only my computer talking to me, I have no complaints. It has been a long, hard road, but I survived and the future looks good. I have come to realize that I don't need to suppress my emotions - be someone who I'm not by hiding my feelings.

I do wonder sometimes how different my life would have been if I hadn't experienced all the abuse. I know parenting doesn't come with a book on how to raise a child, but come on, people, use some common sense.

Give your loved ones a hug and *tell* them how much you love them.

THE FINAL CHAPTER

I understand that some children have endured more mental, emotional and physical abuse than I. I also understand that after reading my autobiography this will bring up bad memories for many of you. Although some will say that after adulthood an adult makes their own choices, I feel that your childhood influences some of the decisions you make throughout your life.

After <u>Suddenly Blind</u> was released for its first printing, it fragmented my family. I have broken off communication with most of them. The harsh words they have directed towards me for bringing this factual story to life is draining. I know that I am not perfect but for me, "The truth will set you free".

There have been many people who have influenced my life or have been friendly acquaintances. Here is an update on their journey through life.

My dear Grandmother Blanche passed away December 3, 2011, eight days prior to me writing this. You held the family together as well as you could. I felt you as you left for your next journey and know Grandpa was there with open arms to embrace you. You and Grandpa Victor are together again, may you both now rest in peace.

Dad passed away in January 2001 from a massive heart attack. The coroner told me, "He was dead before he hit the ground." I have forgiven you and hope that you have found that "something" that you were always searching for.

Mom and Fritz are still together and living comfortably.

The first printing of *Suddenly Blind* has strained our families' relationship. Grandma's death started some sporadic communication between us, but it won't ever be the same.

Ashley, now 24, my daughter, is now re-married and doing fine. We haven't talked in over two years and what I've heard through the grapevine she still resents the way I lost my sight.

My son, Nickolas is now 13 years old and in the eighth grade. We also haven't spoke to each other in two years. He did contact me on Facebook a few months ago but his belligerent attitude towards me prompted me to cut off communication.

Uncle Jim and Aunt Jan now are both retired. They went on to have two children of their own, James and Tara. Brother and Sister, Erik and Erika, are also doing well, and all four have given them grandchildren.

Uncle Johnny and I try to talk regularly and his main concern is what is going to happen to him. He lived with Grandma 99% of his life and will be going to an assisted living center.

My cousin Danny lived a short life. He was killed in an automobile accident around the age of 27. Danny and I had plans on meeting up for a reunion in Omaha where he lived. Time had run out for him before we could make this happen.

My best friend Jim Rogers died at the age of 38 in a motorcycle accident in 2000. Jim went on after our troubled teenage years to marry and have two children. He was living a happy and fulfilling family life until his death.

The last time I spoke with Theresa, my ex-wife, was in 1997. She had battled breast cancer for two years. I suspect she passed away soon after our last conversation as she told me,"I had a rib removed; the cancer is now in my bones." Theresa also had a terrible childhood and couldn't shake off the "ghosts" from her past.

My friend and old landlord, Curt, was struck by a falling tree in 2004 and didn't survive. Debbie, his wife, took Curt's death very hard but has slowly moved on with her life.

I really have no clue about the other people in my book other then Barry and Kathryn. Barry and Kathryn are now proud grandparents and doing well.

As I am going through my final draft of my manuscript I've noticed that most of my friends who I trusted have passed away. I can now count my friends on one hand.

As I'm sitting in the dark I'm pondering this question: *Is the old cliche, "Blood is thicker than water" true?*

I have finally come to the conclusion that, "No, blood is not thicker than water." I have tried all my life to believe that family is always there to trust and fall back on in tough times. I now realize that family members are only people, too. It was much easier for me to forgive and forget negative things my family has done but I've discarded friends if they caused me harm.

Not the case any longer - I now control my life and think of myself and my loved ones first. I've cast away my family members who I can't trust or who have stolen from me.

If I'm not good enough to care about for the last few years, then life goes on without them. I'm finished with them and I'm not willing to have another restless night worrying. I can now lay my head on my pillow and get a good night's sleep.

Holly and I have since shut down our adaptive aids business that provided magnifiers, talking watches, white canes, etc, for the visually impaired/blind. We tried our best to purchase only "Made in the USA" products but it was impossible. We found that most of the products were "Made in China" and were not up to our standards of quality.

We have since taken our frustrations of not being able to purchase goods "Made in the USA" in stores, or manufactured in the USA to creating our documentary, "USA Sticker Shock" (www.usastickershock.com)

The premise of our documentary is to bring jobs back to the USA and be able to purchase quality products again.

My relationship with Holly is going strong and our wedding date is fast approaching. Although the date hasn't been set, we will be married in the spring of 2012. I already know her answer as she has purchased her wedding dress and the rings.

We are planning to purchase a condominium in the next year or two on the beach in Florida and, when money permits, go on cruises and travel around the USA on the train with our guide dogs, Bingo and Oreo.

This Christmas, 2011, Holly and I decided instead of purchasing gifts for everyone, we would take a cruise to Cozumel, Mexico. We lounged together on the deck of the ship for four days and enjoyed most of the entertainment. Now I have "Cruising Fever" and we plan on going on many more cruises during our future days together.

Made in the USA
Charleston, SC
20 February 2013